When Poets Pray

When Poets Pray

Marilyn McEntyre

WILLIAM B. EERDMANS PUBLISHING COMPANY
GRAND RAPIDS, MICHIGAN

Wm. B. Eerdmans Publishing Co.
4035 Park East Court SE, Grand Rapids, Michigan 49546
www.eerdmans.com

25 24 23 22 21 20 19   1 2 3 4 5 6 7

ISBN 978-0-8028-7658-4

Library of Congress Cataloging-in-Publication Data

A catalog record for this book is available from the Library of Congress.

Permission to quote from copyrighted material appears beginning on page 136, which constitutes a continuation of this copyright page.

Contents

Contents

Contents

Witnessing

⟿

Contents

Known and Knowing
⟶ॐ

Introduction

In prayer, as in so many other areas of life, we "learn by going where we have to go." Many of us took our first steps on the path of prayer as children with lines we recited at bedtime or mealtime, or with innocent prayer lists that included blessings for guinea pigs and dolls. We may have come to prayer through crisis or loss, or through those who, when we didn't even realize what we most needed, offered to pray for us.

Those of us who make a practice of prayer probably share an appetite to deepen or open or broaden that practice from time to time. We may want to reach beyond our denominational traditions and learn from those who pray more formally, or less; from those who pray the lectionary, or don't; from those whose prayers are anchored in the liturgical year, or from those whose prayers are freshly called forth like morning dew in the moment. "Teach us to pray" is a prayer to keep praying.

Those who teach us are not always parents or priests or pastors. Sometimes we learn from strangers on street corners whose words stay with us. Sometimes we learn from children, who know how to ask in trust that what they need will be given. Sometimes we learn from poets. Poets have enriched my prayer life by giving me lines that lift up my heart, or words for lament, or images that widen my awareness—of the grandeur of God flaming out "like shining from shook foil," or of a "beauteous evening, calm and free" when "the holy time is quiet as a nun / breathless with adoration."

Poetry and prayer are closely related. Even poems that make no pretense of broaching the sacred invite us to look closely and listen to words, to notice how they trigger associations and invite the mind to play with meaning, how they summon feelings that take us by surprise. Poets slow us down. They teach us to stop and go in before we go on. They play at the edges of mystery, holding a tension between line and sentence, between sense and reason, between the epiphanic and the deeply, comfortingly familiar. Not every poem is a prayer, but I have come to believe that poetry, even for the angry and the disenchanted, takes its inspiration and energy from the Spirit who teaches us to pray.

In the poems and reflections that follow, I take "prayer" to include a range of ways that poets and their readers enter into divine presence. But of course prayer covers a wide range of practices that includes not only words, read or spoken or remembered, recited in a pew or cried out by a deathbed, but also wordless meditation, body work that opens spiritual pathways, the small breath prayers and sudden remembrances that see us through busy days. In the course of those days, words from hymns and Psalms and poems from which only fragments remain in our memories may cross our minds like little comets across the night sky.

The Bible is a rich, essential, and sufficient resource for learning to pray. But it's not a rule book; it is a living word to a living people who are also meant to keep learning from one another in the midst of the long conversation between faith and culture. From those able to articulate current concerns deeply, we learn how to meet the urgencies of our own generation, how to translate, adapt, apply, and live into ancient texts, and how to find words like new wineskins for what the Spirit has done and is doing among us. The fourth-century hymn "Of the Father's Love Begotten" moves me to awe. Lines from a Berkeley poet, wrestling with a life-changing diagnosis in the late twentieth century, do the same: "Let me bless and cherish every moment . . . to arm myself with consciousness / that every earthly darkness / has given way to light, thus far." Another poet wrote, "All love shepherds us." And in their various and beautiful ways, all those who love words shepherd us as well, directing us toward the Word who was in the beginning.

I wrote this book in gratitude. The reflections I offer in the following chapters are my way of giving thanks not only for the poems included, but for many others that have given me phrases, lines, and words that, like little seeds of the Spirit, have taken root and grown and nourished me. I am also grateful, having taught poetry courses over the past three decades, for the ways poets have awakened many who have had no inclination to pray, who find themselves doing something very like praying as something in a turn of phrase turns their hearts in a new direction. Some of the poems I include here are from known poets, others from not-so-known, but each has something to teach us, I think, about how to pray. I have added one of my own poems, not because I think I belong among their ranks, but because I have found myself, on occasion, drawn to pray by means of poems.

I hope that the prayers these poets wrote in quiet moments reclaimed in the midst of their own messy lives may serve contemporary readers in new ways. They redirect us to biblical stories, to images and language in ways that awaken fresh attention. They offer words for situations not unlike those we face, separated though we are from some of them by several hundred years.

All are poets from the "Western tradition," though those of us who inhabit that tradition also have much to learn from the rich spirituality of Asia, Africa, India, and South America, and from tribal cultures everywhere. These poems represent only one lineage among many, but it is one to receive with due regard.

The readings I share here are contemplative exercises, not scholarly analyses. As such, they are meant more as invitation than instruction. My hope is to share gifts I have received from poets who pray, or who reflect on prayer, confident that they have other gifts to deliver to readers who seek in them the spiritual companionship one pilgrim can offer another along the way.

❧ Nature's God ❧

Hildegard of Bingen

From *Meditations*

I am the one whose praise
Echoes on high.

I adorn all the earth.

I am the breeze
That nurtures all things
Green.
I encourage blossoms to flourish with ripening fruits.

I am led by the spirit to feed
The purest streams.

I am the rain
Coming from the dew
That causes the grasses to laugh
With the joy of life.

I call forth tears,
The aroma of holy work.

I am the yearning for good.

It was a long time before I learned that prayer wasn't just talking to God but, more importantly, listening. My first attempts at prayerful listening were frustrating. What I heard was . . . nothing. Then a shift occurred: I discovered a subtle difference between listening *for* and listening *to*. I learned listening as an intentional disposition, attitude, readiness.

Without prepositions, "listen" came to mean something more like open-hearted waiting, breathing, relaxing into wordlessness, becoming aware of Presence. Brother Lawrence, a seventeenth-century French Carmelite, used the phrase "practicing the presence of God." In my efforts at prayerful listening, this phrase acquired new meaning for me. Despite my own intermittent practice over days and years laced with distractions, in the best moments of listening prayer, sometimes a word or phrase or sentence came that I know I didn't "make up." It was given.

As I read the meditations of Hildegard of Bingen, the great twelfth-century mystic and scholar, I am taught again about this dimension of prayer, given in such rich and explicit ways to those folks like me, "busy about many things," who find listening hard to sustain—listening and bearing witness to what we hear. It is there in the prophets. Repeatedly we read that "the word of the Lord came" to Abram, to Jacob, to Moses, to Samuel, to Nathan, to Jehu, to Elijah, to Isaiah and Jeremiah. Their job was to hear and deliver that word.

Of course there are delusions. Distinguishing the word of the Lord from one's own voice, from the internal chatter where memories and plans and desires mingle with bits of poetry, is a little like teasing apart strands in a tangled skein. It behooves any of us, if we think we've heard a message from the Spirit, to check for ego investment, run it by a spiritual director, or otherwise wait for further clarification. But what "comes" in quiet times when our intention is directed toward God is worth our attention.

We can learn about paying that kind of attention from those to whom that word has come, and who have passed it on to us as Hildegard has in her writing. At first she undertook it reluctantly, but finally she opened herself to it as an act of obedience, which was richly rewarded: "I spoke and wrote these things," she recalled, "not by the invention of my heart or that of any other person, but as by the secret mysteries of God I heard and received them in the heavenly places. And again I heard a voice from Heaven saying to me, 'Cry out therefore, and write thus!'" In visions like those above, the voice of God is rendered in simple, brief lines that invite us to pause often and ponder. The God who speaks in them is the same one who uttered forth Creation, and to whom all Creation cries out.

In this short poem, "I am . . . I am . . . I am" echoes like a refrain. It's the name by which God identified God's very self to Moses—a small pronoun and verb which encompass all that is.

My husband has often opened his public prayers with the words "God, you are the one who. . . ." God is the one who provides what we need, or who directs us or holds us or sustains us or gathers us into a living body. I came to love that particular way of entering into prayer—beginning with a reminder and a recognition of who it is we approach when we begin to pray. I imagine how lovely it might be if we paused even in human encounters to look again and say, in effect, "You are the one who opens my mind to points of view I need to hear," or "You are the one who reminds me there is room for laughter, even in hard times," or simply "You are the one I chose and choose again."

In Hildegard's poem, drawn from three volumes of "visionary theology" recorded in similar poetic form, the voice represented as God's invites us first of all to moments of recognition: if we wish to see God, we should look at what happens in the natural world and in humans at their best and most vulnerable. The invitation to see God in dew and rain and blossoms has been reduced to cliché by makers of posters and greeting cards. But mass marketing need not diminish the vision or freshness in this 900-year-old poem. The cloistered woman who wrote it also wrote botany texts and medical treatises and haunting music. In all of it she saw with an open, childlike immediacy what has too often, of late, been flattened into two dimensions and obscured by promiscuous repetition.

The compelling simplicity of her lines invites us back to moments of unveiled awareness. You see the blossom on that branch? It is answering my invitation. Have you noticed how the dew on the grass and the rain keep coming? The great water cycles are one of the many ways I move over the earth and enter into it, and into your very bodies and move among the trout. And among the fluttering aspens. I am verb, not noun. Still, but never static.

Before directing attention to God's presence in the natural world, however, the poem begins with a reminder of God's presence in the heavenly realm. "I am the one whose praise / Echoes on high." We are reminded first and last of God's transcendence. God is beyond what we can observe with the naked, darkened glass of the human eye. To see God in what is near would be misleading if we forgot the cosmic farness and the mystery of the "immortal, invisible" one "whose robe is the light, whose canopy space." God acts from beyond what we know as "nature" and also within and among and through and beneath. So we have ample reason to think of God as both generating and being, as Dylan Thomas put it, "the force that through the green fuse drives the flower."

The "I" in this poem not only calls our attention to who God is, but to what God does, and how to recognize God's work in the world around us. "I adorn," "I encourage," "I cause," "I call forth." Those gentle verbs cover a significant range.

A God who adorns the earth, we are reminded, is a God who delights in beauty, and who, indeed, seems to regard beauty as a necessary dimension of life. I think of how often as a hospice volunteer I have witnessed a hunger for beauty that outlasts even hunger for food. I see it in patients who want flowers or a favorite painting put where they can see it from their bed, or who want to hear music or poems they love. A God who encourages is a God who allows and invites growth, cooperation, and collaboration from humans and all of nature—who invites participation in divine work. A God who causes the grass to laugh with the joy of life is a God who continues to generate a life force that bubbles up like an artesian well even in the smallest life forms. And the God who calls forth is the same who spoke Creation into being, summoning light into darkness and speaking word into silence.

That this God also calls forth tears suggests that our sorrow and our authentic sympathy and pity are likewise forms of participation in the divine life and plan. They open spaces in the heart that can't be opened even by joy. Hildegard's verbs are life-affirming. The list could go on, and her prayer invites us to let it go on, and open doors to faith seeking understanding.

Curiously, one variant among the verbs is a passive construction: "I am led by the spirit to feed / the purest streams." One aspect of God is "led" by another, as though the God of the Trinity includes conversation in community. It reminds us of a family's conversation, where one sibling might tug on another's hand and say, "Look! Over here! Let's move this rock, feed this duck, and put this spider back out where it can live."

The final line of the poem offers a slightly different slant of light. "I am the yearning for good" is a claim of a different kind from those offered in the previous lines. It's one thing to see God's work manifest in the world around us, and even in our tears. It's another to think of our own deepest longings as God-inhabited.

"He will give you the desires of your heart" is a line from the Psalms that shifted for me when I suddenly realized that it meant not only that God would fulfill my desires, but that God would provide the desires themselves, directing and purifying and in some ways complicating them to make them commensurate with what God, in love, might desire for me. Yearning for good is, itself, a gift. It is possible only when the lesser appetites for distractions, personal satisfactions, small victories, and idle pleasures fall away long enough to allow us to discover what it might mean to say, with Augustine, that "our hearts are restless until they rest in thee." Such yearning, even if it's fleeting and quickly fogged over by immediacies, might be a moment of divine encounter devoutly to be wished and prayed for and savored when it's given.

Hildegard invites us to listen, to watch for what comes, and to recognize the force and presence of the giver in the gift—the tree, the stream, the tears, the longing, the poem itself that becomes a prayer in the act of obedient listening and in the bold and trusting work of giving words to what emerges in silence and lingers in the inaudible laughter of grass.

Lucille Clifton

spring song

the green of Jesus
is breaking the ground
and the sweet
smell of delicious Jesus
is opening the house and
the dance of Jesus music
has hold of the air and
the world is turning
in the body of Jesus and
the future is possible

When you repeat the name of Jesus four times in ten very short lines, you mean it. You mean for that name to be noticed and reckoned with—not turned to metaphor or buried behind romantic diminishments of resurrection to the flowers that bloom in the spring (tra-la-la . . .). Clifton does conflate spring and resurrection here, but not by conceding to abstraction. The green of spring grasses and budding branches is "of Jesus" not only in the sense that it belongs to him, but in the sense that he is the "force that through the green fuse drives the flower."

African-American hymns and spirituals, a tradition Clifton claims as an African-American poet and upon which she rings bold changes in this 1987 poem, sing out the name of Jesus in unabashedly intimate, playful, insistent, sometimes wild ways: "A Little Talk with Jesus" will "make it right." "Did You Hear My Jesus" issues a wide invitation to all who are called, because all are called. "Give Me Jesus" claims the only inheritance that matters "when I come to die." "King Jesus" rides in a chariot but walks with those in trials, troubles, and sorrow who sing "I Want Jesus to Walk with Me." Jesus sits "on the waterside" and listens "all day long to hear some sinner pray." And the dying trustfully "steal away to Jesus, . . . steal away home."

To this tradition of trust and full-hearted, full-throated song, Clifton adds "spring song" and other poems that invoke Jesus as the image and likeness of the Creator, who brings forth the fruits of the earth and their fragrances, their buzz and bark and birdsong. Significantly, especially for this gender-aware generation, Jesus is also like a mother, in whose ample womb a new heaven and earth are waiting to be born.

In certain seasons over my years of learning to pray, I've had a hard time addressing myself to Jesus. I could go to God, Creator of the Universe, as I lay under the stars camping, or to the Holy Spirit, in my quietest times, to the intimate, immanent, only a breath and a thought away and not quite so scandalously particular. But Jesus I wrestled with. I grew up with a very culture-specific version of Jesus. The first lullaby I remember was "Trust and Obey," which concluded with the assurance that "there's no other way to be happy in

Jesus but to trust and obey." I stood at my mother's side and sang "What a Friend We Have in Jesus" on prayer-meeting night and "Fairest Lord Jesus" when Easter drew near and "Tell Me the Story of Jesus" before Mom gave one of her lively talks about mission work. I sang "Jesus Loves Me" as a toddler and loved our old 78-rpm record of a men's quartet singing a rousing version of "All Hail the Power of Jesus' Name." I learned the word "prostrate" from that hymn, and "diadem." All of that singing was, I now believe, good faith formation. But, perhaps inevitably, it came to a point where I felt a distance between the Jesus I imagined as I learned Bible verses and pored over the Gospels and the Jesus I encountered as I learned to read more critically and my questions accumulated. Unlike God the Creator and the Holy Spirit, Jesus had a human history recorded in a story full of gaps and strange tonalities and apparent contradictions.

More problematically, the name of Jesus was being used and claimed by televangelists and other very public people in alienating and troubling ways. Their Jesus wasn't my Jesus, whoever mine was. I registered with belated shock the obvious fact that Jesus wasn't white, but born into an ancient, somewhat alien culture whose norms I found puzzling, and that Christians of a certain bent were inclined to airbrush out his inconvenient edges, oversimplify his message and the meaning of his life, and make him in their image.

Part of the grace of Trinitarian faith is that we can address God under more than one aspect, taking refuge in one when another is undergoing theological scrutiny. But eventually that same Trinitarian doctrine requires that we come to terms with whatever aspect of God, or particular claims about God, we've been avoiding. I was summoned back in very specific ways to Jesus.

One moment of summoning came when I visited the Metropolitan Museum of Art in New York. Tired of graduate studies, I had taken the train into the city for an unusual afternoon of solitude. I found my way to the special exhibit of Russian icons, having been told it was not to be missed. I was looking at one after another, trying to recall what I had learned about them in my art history course, about how they're meant to be looked at not aesthetically, but devotionally, how they're meant to become portals to divine encounter. Ready to move away from one of the many figures of the divine Mother and Child, I turned and suddenly found myself riveted by a face of Jesus across the room. It was, I still believe, the most striking—no, stunning—experience I'd ever had in an art museum. I walked across the room as though I had been summoned by name and stood in front of the image of Jesus, meeting the dark eyes and finding that they indeed opened a way into what felt for a moment like direct encounter with divine presence. I didn't levitate. I didn't even kneel and pray, but I did stand there for quite some time, consenting to whatever mysterious bidding was being given. I remembered Jesus's words to Paul: "I am Jesus, whom you are persecuting." I wasn't, I hasten to add, persecuting him, but I was avoiding him. And that image troubled me into changing course. I began intermittently—between exams and research papers—to read the Gospels again slowly, a little more open-heartedly, asking for guidance and grace.

Those came early one morning when I had risen to do the exercises I wish I still had the stamina and will to do regularly. Right in the middle of bending and stretching, I "heard," though not in my ears, "Read the Gospel of John." The imperative was so sudden and forceful that I stopped the music, went to the bookcase, and pulled out the Bible that had again languished for some time. "In the beginning was the Word," I read, "and the Word was with God and the Word was God." An image of Jesus not unlike the icon in New York seemed to occupy space in the room. I realized I was being called, and Jesus was doing the calling.

The third experience came in my practice of centering prayer. I was breathing slowly, waiting for a word to come that would be my centering word, trying out "peace" and "here" and "open heart," but what came was "Jesus." I have to admit, I had been veering away from it. The name of Jesus was too fraught with personal history, theology, and oblique associations I imagined would be distracting. But insistently the name came back: Jesus. You want to enter into centering prayer today? This name is your anchor.

And so it is. Lucille Clifton's poem delights me in its unabashed joy in Jesus—"delicious" Jesus! In all my years of singing and speaking and reading about Jesus, I had not encountered that descriptor, or the notion that Jesus music "has hold of the air," though African-American gospel choirs have certainly justified that vivid, palpable description of what happens when a sacred song takes over the whole body and becomes a dance. The poem is a testimony to the power of that "Jesus music," and to the hope that Jesus people have borne into the world in every generation, despite the Inquisitors and the Crusaders and the punishers and the warmongers and the next-generation pharisees who use his name as a market label. In this poem, the name of Jesus isn't an instrument of division, but something like a drumbeat, summoning all those within its hearing to dwell in divine possibility.

Walter Chalmers Smith

Immortal, Invisible, God Only Wise

Immortal, invisible, God only wise,
In light inaccessible hid from our eyes,
Most blessèd, most glorious, the Ancient of Days,
Almighty, victorious, thy great Name we praise.

Unresting, unhasting, and silent as light,
Nor wanting, nor wasting, thou rulest in might;
Thy justice like mountains high soaring above
Thy clouds which are fountains of goodness and love.

To all life thou givest—to both great and small;
In all life thou livest, the true life of all;
We blossom and flourish as leaves on the tree,
And wither and perish—but naught changeth thee.

Great Father of glory, pure Father of light,
Thine angels adore thee, all veiling their sight;
All laud we would render: O help us to see
'Tis only the splendor of light hideth thee.

When a prayer is a poem, it often invites music. The adage that "those who sing once pray twice" reminds us of how music enhances both prayer and poetry. Any number of hymns might be included in these reflections on poets' prayers. I think, for instance, of a few that take me directly into prayer every time I sing them: "Be Thou My Vision," "Of the Father's Love Begotten," "Come, Thou Fount of Every Blessing." Many hymns are musical settings of poems written as individual prayers, some on dire occasions, like "If Thou but Trusted God to Guide Thee" and "It Is Well with My Soul." And of course the texts of many spirituals that come from the singing of African-American slaves are poems in which rhythm and repetition crescendo into confidence and proclamation.

It was said of Walter Chalmers Smith, a nineteenth-century Scottish Free Church pastor, that poetry was "the retreat of his nature from the burden of his labors."* Like Hildegard's, his poetry seems to have been integral to his prayer life, in which intimacy and awe reflected the great paradox that God the Creator, though "above all things," also dwells "in all things," animating the natural world, and dwelling more deeply within us than our own beating hearts. "Immortal, Invisible," written in 1867, is only one of the many poems in the eleven volumes that Smith wrote during his active years of ministry between 1860 and 1893. It is his best known, having survived as a beloved and familiar hymn that has provided a beautiful reminder of the immensity and glory of the God who created, and whose Spirit infuses all things.

* See https://www.umcdiscipleship.org.

The first and last stanzas of this hymn focus on God's transcendence, splendor, majesty, mystery, omnipotence—God as light, the Source and End of all energy, power, and love. These are large thoughts; they call us to open the contemplative reach of our imaginations with metaphors that allow some access to omnipotent, omniscient divinity, with special emphasis on light—ambient, pervasive, surrounding and suffusing, quietly, powerfully present, unseen because it is that by which we see.

I remember a sermon in which the pastor pointed out that there are only two "God is" statements in Scripture: God is love, and God is light. Light seems to have a special status, lifting it a little beyond metaphor and inviting us to recognize in what we know about light something about the nature of God—including the fact that only a small portion of its wavelengths are visible to the human eye. We are wrapped in light as we are wrapped in love; both are forms of energy that fuel life.

I think that my favorite phrase in the hymn is "Unresting, unhasting, and silent as light." This lovely line, slowed by commas that invite us to linger over the slightly antique descriptors, helps me to relax into the truth that God is not the author of "noise and haste," but of the slow emergence, of the unfolding, evolving of things, of a created order that brings forth its fruit in "due season," and of the great quiet that is the source and origin of all utterance.

And of all life: "To all life thou givest, to both great and small." I think of this line when I see small animals who have met their death in the wild or on the roads that crisscross their habitats, and when I see new shoots in the garden. That all life is a gift is a truth to return to with every new morning and every meal. But the next line adds a dimension to that very human understanding of what is given: "In all life thou livest, the true life of all." God not only gives, but *is* the gift. In God we live and move and have our being. Jesus's mysterious words in the farewell discourses of John, "Abide in me and I in you," remind us that we participate in divine life, draw upon the life source with every breath, and cannot be separated from the One whose we are in life and in death.

The hymn ends with a petition I love for the way it brings me back to awareness of the God "whose presence is everywhere": "O help us to see / 'Tis only the splendor of light hideth thee." The paradox is both profound and playful: light reveals; darkness hides. But to consider that God is hidden in the light is to recognize what Einstein hinted at when he mused, "Subtle is the Lord."

In our breath, in the folding of our proteins and the replication of our cells, in the great quiet that astronauts enter as they leave our noisy planet, in the music that shapes us ("and you are the music while the music lasts") and echoes after the final note, in the light that wraps us by day and the darkness by night, God is here and now, present and incomprehensible, immanent and transcendent, intimate and unknowable, immortal, invisible. And this good news is new every morning.

Robert Frost

A Prayer in Spring

Oh, give us pleasure in the flowers today;
And give us not to think so far away
As the uncertain harvest; keep us here
All simply in the springing of the year.

Oh, give us pleasure in the orchard white,
Like nothing else by day, like ghosts by night;
And make us happy in the happy bees,
The swarm dilating round the perfect trees.

And make us happy in the darting bird
That suddenly above the bees is heard,
The meteor that thrusts in with needle bill,
And off a blossom in mid air stands still.

For this is love and nothing else is love,
To which it is reserved for God above
To sanctify to what far ends he will,
But which it only needs that we fulfill.

This 1915 poem, unusual among Frost's poems for its light, lilting, simple joy in the natural world, leads me not only to his other New England poems—"After Apple Picking," "Birches"—but also to a poet who is among his worthiest successors—Wendell Berry. To begin reflection on one poet by admiring another is, I suppose, a way of acknowledging that poetry is an ongoing conversation whose threads are tucked and woven into a design that no one poet knows or needs to know. As I return to Frost's "Prayer in Spring," I can't help hearing Wendell Berry's lovely lines, written over half a century later, as a kind of echo of the older poem:

> And we pray, not
> for new earth or heaven, but to be
> quiet in heart, and in eye,
> clear. What we need is here.

One of the functions of prayer is to bring us into the present. Whatever the prayer posture we assume—bowed head and closed eyes, hands lifted or open in our laps—the small discipline of quieting body and mind is how we commonly "come into the presence" of God, who is always present, and into the present moment. It may be that the concerns we bring into prayer include past hurts and anxieties that tug our dark imaginations toward a dark future, but to pray is to locate ourselves in "this day," where the daily bread we need is all we need to pray for.

The petition that opens Frost's "Prayer in Spring" appears to be a modest one: "pleasure in the flowers today" seems little enough to ask, especially on a spring morning in New England when that pleasure would seem inevitable. But to make the petition is to recognize that our capacity for such pleasure isn't to be taken for granted. If we are among the many modern folk whom T. S. Eliot recognized as "distracted from distraction by distraction," pausing to notice the peonies in the garden or the alyssum by the sidewalk's edge or the wild roses clinging to a neighbor's fence might require a release from compulsion that we can't achieve entirely by will. Hurry is a hard habit to break, and noticing is a discipline easily eroded.

To pray for pleasure like this is to pray for the grace of undivided attention and the childlike astonishment that recognizes the flame-like petals of this particular rose as a new thing on earth, given only to this flower, this day, available this time, for me, because I am here. "Beauty and grace are performed whether or not we will or sense them," Annie Dillard writes. "The least we can do is try to be there." But being there may be more than we can manage without the particular gift of sight and open heart Frost prayed for one spring day.

This poem is also a prayer for protection from the fears that drain our energies and unsettle our hearts. Worry about the uncertain harvest may be a New England farmer's besetting anxiety, but it serves to remind any of us of those endeavors we have to prepare, plant, water, and then leave to God and nature to complete. Raising children or bearing them. Presenting a project proposal. Investing an inheritance. Teaching a class full of squirrely twelve-year-olds. Caring for a beloved one whose prognosis is unclear. Freedom from fear was a noble hope when Roosevelt included it among the "four freedoms" he aspired to on behalf of all Americans, but it can't be simply declared or claimed; it has to be received, and the fear dispelled, through the Spirit who saves us, again and again, from ourselves. In one guise or another, we need the angel who shows up to show up again and again to say, "Be not afraid."

Only when we're free from besetting fear can we "be happy in the happy bees." The preposition here that denotes such a very particular happiness—not as happy *as* the bees, nor happy *like* the bees, nor happy *about* or *with* or (if you're allergic and skittish about bees) *in spite of* them, but happy *in* the bees. Happy about the very fact of bees in the world, and us among them, recognizing the bees as a factor in our happiness, and—though this seems perhaps less likely—us in theirs. To pray for this kind of happiness is to seek deep and authentic contentment in what is—the created order as it was given. Contentment may seem a pale thing to desire compared to excitement or adventure or innovation—at least to the very young—but it deserves to be reclaimed as a state of mind and heart "devoutly to be wished." Contentment is an alignment of our will with God's will as we understand it.

Contentment makes room for small pleasures like watching a hummingbird dart and drink and hover—a pleasure to which the whole of the third stanza is devoted. I remember my mother's calling me to the kitchen window to watch a hummingbird feed. Though they were not an unusual sight, each one of them gave her a few moments of visible delight. She loved them. She seemed to deem it a privilege to see them, as though being allowed into their world and business as a visitor was not to be taken for granted. The stillness of the hummingbird in midair offers its own particular fascination. What is it waiting for? Thinking? Or doing just there before it dives into the next flower or flies off to its nesting place? An ornithologist would offer a fair explanation of its behavior, but wouldn't finally penetrate the mystery of otherness that is part of what makes one happy in the hummingbirds.

That happiness—contentment in connection with other crea-
tures, acceptance of the distance between us and of the permission
a moment gives to pause and draw near to them and find ourselves
alive in the same great mystery—is love. Whether or not that love
is divine, the speaker suggests, is not really our business. God's
purposes are God's. Our part is to say yes to what is given, grate-
fully, giving it due attention, without the presumption of posses-
sion. The poem specifically unlinks possession from happiness,
praying rather for a happiness that is love because it doesn't need
to possess, but only to enjoy.

The old catechisms teach that our chief end is "to glorify God
and enjoy him forever." "Glorify" is a large word, but it may be that
its meaning lies very close to the simple matter of true enjoyment—
the kind that breaks forth when a child points to a feather or a falling
star and cries, "Oh! Look!" There is happiness in noticing. Noticing
begets a love that, as the speaker rightly says, is up to God to sanctify.

"A Prayer in Spring" is not the prayer of an ascetic or a puritan.
Its frank focus on pleasure at the beginning, then happiness, then
love links the three in a way which reminds us that pleasure is
good, and that pleasure is an important dimension of worship. It
may be that the term "pleasure" has suffered by frequent associa-
tion with the pleasures of the flesh or idle pleasures that sate but
do not satisfy. But this poem restores the word to its rightful place
among those long elevated to liturgical use, like gladness ("with
gladness and singleness of heart") and joy ("that our joy may be
complete"). Pleasure is worth praying for because so much of mass
culture militates against the slow and simple pleasures that spring-
time affords. We need pleasure. We need to sustain in ourselves the
capacity for pleasure. And so we pray for pleasure in these flowers,
this day.

Wendell Berry

Prayer after Eating

I have taken in the light
that quickened eye and leaf.
May my brain be bright with praise
of what I eat, in the brief blaze
of motion and of thought.
May I be worthy of my meat.

I love the simple ritual of grace before meals. Preceded and followed by a slow, long, intentional breath that releases the day's distractions and allows us to relax into the simple pleasures of gathering and eating, it seems a little like lighting a candle whose light changes the whole room. Many families continue to say grace before meals even when other faith practices have dwindled to holiday rituals. Where that is the case, that one quiet moment of turning toward God as the source of life and health and blessing assumes particular significance, even if it is brief and rote. I still occasionally think of the first mealtime grace I learned about the time I began to speak: "God is great and God is good, and we thank him for our food." These days, I'm more inclined to acknowledge the many layers of human labor, some of it undercompensated, that are the costs of our abundant fare, and to ask for food to be produced more justly and wisely, but God's greatness and goodness still seem something to be acknowledged before eating, and I'm grateful for the little prayer that opened my imagination to awareness of blessing—that it keeps coming, that what lies before us here, now, is blessing.

Wendell Berry's "Prayer after Eating," written in 1971 and widely shared since then, reminds us of a custom less widely retained: of giving thanks after as well as before a meal, framing the whole event in a way that sets it apart as sacred time, as space separate from the other enterprises of the day, to be entered into and left with reverence. But it does much more than that. This deceptively brief prayer invites us to a level of reflection that is easy to avoid: it reminds us of the deep biological processes in which we are intricately involved, how light becomes food, and food becomes flesh. It reminds us that food fuels not only the flesh, but also the brain that apprehends and the affective life that enables us to be grateful. It reminds us of our mortality: that life is a "brief blaze." That stark but wonderful image of what burns in the night—a comet, a fire in the hearth, a twinkling star—invites us to imagine our short lives here as something shockingly beautiful, "charged," as Hopkins put it, "with the grandeur of God" for one brief, shining moment.

But the prayer doesn't end on that dramatic note; instead, it concludes with a simple petition: "May I be worthy of my meat." Blessing is freely and abundantly given, whether we acknowledge it or not, but when we do, it behooves us to recognize what we commonly call a "debt of gratitude." It leaves us with something to rise to. Most of us, I imagine, received some form of early training intended to move us beyond the self-centeredness necessary to mere survival into the realm of grace and generosity. Most of us were told that a right response to our privilege and ease was to share it. And most of us who grew up in Christian homes heard versions of the Sermon on the Mount periodically that reminded us of the cup of water, the bread, the fish, the cloak we owed the poor. And most of us, I imagine, still need those prompts to maintain the measure of humility it takes to recognize, as the centurion did, that we are, of ourselves, unworthy. That only God can make us worthy.

To be made worthy of my meat would be, perhaps, to go out into the world with deepened concern for those who harvested or packaged or loaded and transported food from farms to our table (concern Berry has expressed with the unusual depth of understanding he brings to each of those populations as a farmer, man of faith, social critic, and environmentalist). It would be to assume responsibility, not in a spirit of guilt but in a spirit of gladness, for giving back where I have received, not only in caring for other human beings, but for the soil, the water, the air, taking an active interest in the health of ecosystems and the species that sustain them. All that takes time and care and conversation. Being made worthy, as the verb suggests, isn't something we can do alone, but only with God's help and each other's. God's help has already been given; grace abounds. What remains for us to do is to educate and encourage one another toward humble, intelligent stewardship and responsible consumption that begins and ends in gratitude.

Joy Harjo

Eagle Poem

To pray you open your whole self
To sky, to earth, to sun, to moon
To one whole voice that is you.
And know there is more
That you can't see, can't hear;
Can't know except in moments
Steadily growing, and in languages
That aren't always sound but other
Circles of motion.
Like eagle that Sunday morning
Over Salt River. Circled in blue sky
In wind, swept our hearts clean
With sacred wings.
We see you, see ourselves and know
That we must take the utmost care
And kindness in all things.
Breathe in, knowing we are made of
All this, and breathe, knowing
We are truly blessed because we
Were born, and die soon within a

True circle of motion,
Like eagle rounding out the morning
Inside us.
We pray that it will be done
In beauty.
In beauty.

Enacting in its own beauty what it prays for, "Eagle Poem" reminds us that prayer is something heard, received, and lived before it is distilled into words. The Spirit dwells within us, we are taught—a truth that not only Christians but people of most faith traditions believe: God speaks in the still, small voice of conscience, of prompting, a voice within us, teaching and reminding and inviting. Prayers come as, by most poets' accounts, poems come—given, at least in raw form, to be crafted with a humility we might well call obedience. Harjo, a contemporary poet of the Muskogee (Creek) nation, says of her own work, "I'm still amazed. And I still say, after writing poetry for all this time, and now music, that ultimately humans have a small hand in it. We serve it. We have to put ourselves in the way of it, and get out of the way of ourselves."*

What might it mean to "put ourselves in the way of" prayer? The poem offers one answer: "open your whole self / To sky, to earth, to sun, to moon / To one whole voice that is you. / And know there is more. . . ." To pray is to open up prayer space and let prayer happen, patiently, without too quickly filling that space

* See the interview at poetryfoundation.org.

with words, to allow information and invitation to come from any direction—from the cosmos, from the self, from the world of plants and animals that teach us things by their ways of being, at once complex and innocent. I think of the animals in Scripture that were appointed as bearers of God's message: the dove, the donkey, the cock, the eagle. Those that figure in historical scenes and those used for poetic effect ("they shall mount up on wings like eagles") together serve to remind us that animals have special places as servants and signs in both the divine and natural order.

More than once I've heard stories from friends about how, in the days following the death of a beloved friend or family member, a bird appeared at an unusual time or in an unusual way, as though a sign that all was well. They took comfort from those gulls, pelicans, or unseasonal robins they believed were messengers. These stories and the evidence from generations and traditions of human testimony indicate that God may speak through nature directly and personally when we are attentive.

The poem's specificity about "that Sunday morning" locates the eagle's flight in time—not just in legend or lore. Written in 1990, the poet's words carry within them seeds of a long tribal tradition as well as an acute consciousness of the historical moment in which this prayer is offered. This is the way of biblical stories—*this* mountain, *this* slave girl, *this* fig tree, *this* road, horse, man, moment. In prayer we are met. Encounters with God may happen when we set out to pray, but also when we do not: our disinclinations put no limit on God's purposes. And when we are met, our hearts may be "swept clean."

The poem ends with a lovely, urgent, emphatic repetition, asking that our lives be accomplished and made whole "In beauty. / In beauty." That beauty is to be prayed for, and that beauty is to be sought and found in prayer is an understanding many of us need to reclaim. This Creek prayer, like many prayers from Native American traditions, is slow and deliberate, making ample space for pause and breath, keeping lines short and strong, ending with a phrase that echoes like a drumbeat. In Ecclesiastes we read, "He has made everything beautiful in its time"; in the Psalms, that "His holy mountain, beautiful in elevation, is the joy of all the earth." And Isaiah prophesies, "In that day the branch of the LORD shall be beautiful and glorious. . . ." God's way is one of beauty, and all beauty points to its Source in the heart of the Creator. So it is right that prayer be made beautiful, that it call our attention to beauty, and that beautiful lives and the beauty that feeds and teaches us are goods for which we are right to pray.

❧ Wrestling ❧

John Donne

Holy Sonnet XIV

Batter my heart, three-person'd God, for you
As yet but knock, breathe, shine, and seek to mend;
That I may rise and stand, o'erthrow me, and bend
Your force to break, blow, burn, and make me new.
I, like an usurp'd town to another due,
Labor to admit you, but O, to no end;
Reason, your viceroy in me, me should defend,
But is captiv'd, and proves weak or untrue.
Yet dearly I love you, and would be lov'd fain,
But am betroth'd unto your enemy;
Divorce me, untie or break that knot again,
Take me to you, imprison me, for I,
Except you enthrall me, never shall be free,
Nor ever chaste, except you ravish me.

I first encountered this strange, strenuous seventeenth-century poem in a college classroom, as many do—not a particularly fitting context in which to receive and reflect on its spiritual challenge. But I had the good fortune to be guided through it by an inspiring professor whose great literary passion was the seventeenth-century "metaphysical" poets, John Donne chief among them. The professor himself was a bit outlandish and wild-eyed, given to extravagant claims and edgy anecdotes. So he was a fitting guide: he taught us to love Donne's paradoxes, the tensions and stresses in the poem, the brash improprieties and disturbing metaphors, not simply because they were outrageous, but because they were theologically appropriate. Donne, a notorious rake and womanizer in his younger years, came to his belated vocation as Anglican priest with a spirit of repentance and an exuberant gratitude that matched his other passions in urgency and magnitude of feeling.

Roughly paraphrased, the poem confesses something like this. I am a slave to sin; my heart is fickle and deceitful. There's no way I'm going to come back to you, God, if you don't wrench me by force from the devil's stronghold and invade my deepest inner places. It is, we can assume, a real confession of a real man: Donne was pretty candid about his personal knowledge of sin and temptation. And the argument of the poem rests on good Reformation theology: only God can redeem and repair us; we can't do it for ourselves. It gets at the desperate nature of addiction, uncontrolled appetite, and ego possession.

But it gets at those things in unnerving ways. It was a shock at the time to learn that "ravish" actually meant rape. "Ravish" is a rather appealing word if you don't know what it means—it sounds domestic and cheerful like "radish," or inviting like "relish," or a bit ironic, like "rubbish," the British term of dismissal. . . . But when you recognize that it means to abduct by force and generally implies rape, this poem turns very dark. My own first encounter with the final lines of Holy Sonnet XIV was every bit as shocking as Donne apparently intended. At the time I first studied it, I was also beginning to read the mystics and was struck by how often they, too, borrowed erotic words to speak of encounter with God. Their language unsettled me. So, for that matter, did The Song of Songs.

That "ravish" also means "to overwhelm with emotion; enrapture," though, serves Donne's purposes perfectly. His purposes are a lot like those of Flannery O'Connor, who frequently resorted to shocking images to get at the magnitude of sin and the extraordinary nature of radical grace.

"Sin" is an unpopular word, and a sense of its horror is hard to sustain when we so commonly domesticate our bad habits, excuse our errant ways, and regard our foibles with affectionate irony. We have (rightly, I think) reclassified some "sins" as psychopathologies. What some of us were taught to regard as personal sins may in fact be systemic: people may be driven to push drugs by poverty created by other people's greed. Conviction of personal sin in our complicated, secularized culture can become so highly modified that we no longer feel much urgency about escaping it. We may be among the "good people" that Flannery O'Connor acerbically recognized as inured to grace and in need of a rude awakening.

Donne tries one metaphor after another in an effort to get at what sin is. We are like dented and damaged vessels that can't be made usable by patching or polish, but have to be melted and recast—reduced and reformed in the most literal sense. Or we are like towns taken over by enemy forces. Our defenses against grace have become militant and violent. We are like slaves who have lost even the will to seek freedom. We are like brides given in unholy marriage to abusive husbands. We are bound by a Gordian knot that God alone can untie. The forms of damage, abjection, and addiction suggested here are dire, but, interestingly, they are not willful. We've been cracked and broken and need to be fixed, caught and need to be freed, hurt and need to be healed.

It can be tempting, in light of its violent images, to write off the poem as evidence of Donne's bad taste. Fortunately, though, my teacher knew enough theology and cultural history, and had developed enough informed sympathy for the profundity of Donne's penitence to enable us to appreciate why he would choose such extreme metaphors to make his point. They actually offer compassionate rather than punitive ways of thinking about what sin is. I think as I read the poem of the wisdom so many have found in twelve-step programs. There, along with being required to acknowledge the damage done to others, addicts understand themselves as captives of compulsions that can't be overcome by will alone but only by prayer, shared accountability, and love.

That message of compassion deepens even as the last couplet complicates it. But the final paradox, the one I found so difficult at first, challenges us to imagine God's grace in even starker terms: "nor ever chaste, except you ravish me." How shall I be purified except by giving myself completely, allowing myself to be taken over, occupied, enraptured by the One whom another poet called "this tremendous Lover"?

I have come increasingly to love and rely on this poem. I have come back to it, grateful, in my own moments of sorrow, for precisely that unsparing reminder of ways my own heart has been hardened and has needed to be "battered" like a closed door. It can't be reduced to a display of clever poetic devices. The opening imperative is every bit as urgent as the Psalmist's "O LORD, make haste to help me!" Followed by "Three-person'd God," it enlists the entire Trinity to do the job. Every dimension of divine power is invoked to save what is almost utterly lost. Behind the words I hear the echo of Luther's insistence that an adequate understanding of what Christ undertook requires an effort to fathom the depth and horror of sin.

Over the years those lines have lost, perhaps from much teaching, some of their shock value. But they still awaken longing: I want to desire God this urgently—God who gives us the very desires of our hearts, not just the objects of those desires. I have longed to be as fully possessed as St. Catherine in ecstasy, or St. Teresa in prayer. To be caught up, taken up, held, possessed, and inhabited by Love itself is a good thing to want—the best thing.

It is possible to find in this poem, and in the prayer it prays so fervently, an invitation to imagine divine love, and to discover a desire that is the beginning of its own fulfillment. It opens, like any prayer prayed from the heart, a way to what it asks.

Gerard Manley Hopkins

Thou Art Indeed Just, Lord

Justus quidem tu es, Domine, si disputem tecum;
verumtamen justa loquar ad te: Quare via impiorum
  prosperatur?

Thou art indeed just, Lord, if I contend
With thee; but, sir, so what I plead is just.
Why do sinners' ways prosper? And why must
Disappointment all I endeavour end?
Wert thou my enemy, O thou my friend,
How wouldst thou worse, I wonder, than thou dost
Defeat, thwart me? O, the sots and thralls of lust
Do in spare hours more thrive than I that spend,
Sir, life upon thy cause. See, banks and brakes
Now, leaved how thick! Laced they are again
With fretty chervil, look, and fresh wind shakes
Them; birds build—but not I build; no, but strain,
Time's eunuch, and not breed one work that wakes.
Mine, O thou lord of life, send my roots rain.

I don't know of any other prayer that addresses God as "Sir." This dark and difficult sonnet, written in 1888 after five years that seemed to the poet dry and wasted, articulates discouragement, desperation, frustration, and spiritual exhaustion with dark and disturbing accuracy. But that little address in the second line always makes me smile. I imagine the speaker drawing himself up to full height, straightening his cravat (not a tie—this is the nineteenth century, and Oxford) and waistcoat, and facing the divine Judge like a lawyer ready to make his case. And he has a case: he is pleading a just cause. Some things just aren't fair. And he has confidence in the justice of the judge, so the poem, bleak as it becomes, begins with assurance and a sturdy faith that has survived the thwarting and defeat and jealousies that assail the weary plaintiff. So he begins with a clear if disgruntled declaration of that faith: God is indeed just. However, the "but" clause that follows thrusts the other prong of paradox into the poem like a pitchfork. If we're required to believe that God is just, responsive to our prayers, one who honors our efforts and sends the Spirit to sustain our faith, what do we do with fruitlessness, fatigue, and unwarranted failure?

Recently I heard on public radio a program devoted to stories of failure. One of them stood out as unusually honest, as this poem is: the writer admitted that she had no final success story that would make her story of failure into a parable or an encouraging teaching tale. What failed, failed. She picked up and went on, but had found as yet no obvious redemptive value in the experience. She did tell her story with simplicity and eloquence that seemed to me itself to be a gift plucked from the ruins she described. We need those stories, too. We need to know that bad things often just sit there like burnt trees on the hillside, signs of loss. Eventually, as the story gets longer, as life goes on and shadow and light mingle in a more complicated design, we may find ourselves on new plateaus of understanding. In the meantime, failure looks a lot like failure, and we may feel we are being, as Yeats put it, "bred to a harder thing than Triumph."

The common and reasonable questions raised in the poem's third and fourth lines might sound peevish—a bit of a whine, especially since it's hard not to hear the "all" as the kind of hyperbole that petulant children or fed-up adults resort to when they want to make a point. One imagines the plaintiff in his professional garb just barely restrained enough to resist stamping his foot. He does, in fact, hit the stressed syllables in the iambic pentameter particularly hard in this line. And then his complaint becomes more bitter, and his lament more poignant: "Wert thou my enemy, O thou my friend, / How wouldst thou worse, I wonder, than thou dost / defeat, thwart me?" Or, as we have doubtless heard the question in more colloquial circumstances, "With friends like you, who needs enemies?" Yet the poem holds us to the paradox; the speaker breaks his slide into simple bitterness with an interruption that seems to come from a breaking heart: "O thou my friend" goes a good way further even than the opening concession that God is indeed just. God, in Christ, is the One who called us friends. Even in the midst of near despair, even as he rails, the speaker remembers and clings to that bond.

He imagines (if he can't see them out his leaded window roaming the streets of his ancient university town) addicts ("sots") and prostitutes and their patrons ("thralls of lust"). They seem to go unpunished by remorse or disease—they eat well, enjoy laughter, and even remain healthy in the midst of slow self-destruction. It's a familiar feeling; I think of the barrage of glamour magazines, films, and celebrity events that feature what we now call the one percent looking their fit and beautiful best, who seem favored by fortune beyond all reasonable measure. Even if we know what a masquerade it all is, envy comes easily, and occasions for it are ubiquitous. The habit of comparison is hard to avoid.

My husband often quotes a friend who reminded him, in moments of emergent professional envy, "There's no competition in the kingdom of heaven." It is the message of Rabbi Zusya, who tells his congregation that when he stands before God, he will not be asked, "Why were you not Moses?" but "Why were you not Zusya?" Comparison and competition in spiritual life don't end well. But they aren't just bad habits to be shaken off. They run deep along our interior fault lines.

The speaker in this poem, like many among us who might bang their fists on desks where sermons are being prepared or on tables where food is being served to the hurried and ungrateful, is one who has dedicated his life to God. And God's rewards seem, at least in this bleak moment, to remain behind a cloudbank. No illumination. No transformation. No mystical moments. Not to mention money, recognition, or intimate companionship. Hopkins, a Jesuit and an academic, must have felt these lacks keenly on winter days in the chilly English Midlands, where he suffered from severe gastro-intestinal afflictions, bleeding, and weakness even as he prepared the lectures and wrote the poems that have comforted generations of the afflicted.

Even in springtime, when the "banks and brakes" are in full leaf and the trees in blossom, when birds build their nests, it feels to this exhausted soul as though all nature mocks him in its resilient abundance. The lusty month of May holds no charms for this young Jesuit, a devout convert to Roman Catholicism: he finds himself out of step, out of tune, and deeply out of sorts even when spring and divine love encircle him with beauty and promise. He is "time's eunuch," incapable, he believes, of transmitting life, or even the liveliness of work done well and shared, bound in lifetime servitude that seems, in this moment, utterly sterile.

Most of us have been there. When the work of a morning or a month seems wasted or our efforts appear undone by circumstances beyond our control; when—as happened to several friends—manuscripts are burned in house fires or artworks that were labors of love are lost in transit. We need time to grieve these losses. This poet knows that. Thirteen of the sonnet's fourteen lurching lines are given to lament. But in the end we come to a prayer so simple and pure, so utterly given over to the God whose justice is inscrutable and whose love is unsearchable, that the lament returns to trust like waves returning to the sea. It is the prayer of a man who knows the ways of the natural world—that water must reach the deep roots to feed the living tree. That it comes when it will, in God's time, not ours. That it will come, as it has come. "Mine, O thou lord of life, send my roots rain" is a prayer that returns to me in my own most desiccated moments, and one for which I have had reason repeatedly to be thankful. As I am for the whole poem, for the way it honors the uneasy relationship of feeling to faith, for its odd, endearing formalities, for its impulsive moments of yielding to love even in the midst of outrage, for its emotional honesty and its poetic complexity.

That last, by the way, is part of its teaching. To honor the complexity of the truth one tells is the task of a good poet—to find, as Wallace Stevens put it, "what will suffice." Hopkins's prayer is a sonnet for good reason: a sonnet is traditionally a love poem.

Though it has been turned to other purposes, often for the sake of irony, it is, first and always, an address to or reflection on the beloved. And so this sonnet is. The Lord of life who is "mine," "my friend," and a just judge is also the One who gives us, because we need even this, roots whose thirst drives us back to prayer.

SAID

Psalm

From *99 Psalms*
Translated from the German by Mark S. Burrows

[13]
lord
pray
pray aloud against the clamor of the human hand
that seeks to drown you out
and appear on quiet soles
so that we might understand your footsteps
strive
to acknowledge our prayers
even when they appear in some other guise
for no prayer ever unbinds itself from its origins
with the one who prays

[14]
lord
take up the speech
by which i pray to you
grant me the gestures

that have grown within me in your absence
that i might remain true to my incorrigible nature
and take up your weakness

[22]
lord
keep on wandering forever and never
settle down
because no dwelling places remain
only footsteps
be loud and urgent
share in my life and my passions
accompany me
all the way to your bread
so that my word might wake

[25]
lord
stay with me
even when i nourish myself from ashes and salt
be still and listen to each of the names
i lend you
for i want to distinguish you from the false gods
give me patience to endure the vain
with their empty words
and the converts
who strive to confirm their opposite
and make
my waiting full of revolt

[31]
lord
when you arrive
we'll be light
bread and water
the table is set and the door ajar
come and be seated among us
free me of the belief
that you're only faithful from a distance
and speak with me
in the unharried speech of animals
who watch us from afar
with their unadulterated hunger

Occasionally, over the years, I've puzzled over the use of imperatives. "Come, Lord . . . ," "Speak, Lord . . . ," "Answer me . . . ," "Incline your ear . . . ," "Open my lips . . . ," "Show me . . . ," "Teach me . . . ," and so on. The Psalms are full of them—outcries, often, or sometimes exuberant invitations. "Imperative" is, after all, a grammatical term, not necessarily a peremptory attitude or posture. Still, sometimes it seems as though there's something a little presumptuous about directing or demanding God's attention.

The imperatives in SAID's short psalms push the envelope. The poet, an Iranian who immigrated to Germany as an engineering student and remained to become one of Germany's most noted contemporary poets, challenges readers on several counts. His collection of 99 psalms, one reviewer pointed out, invites "adherents of at least three Abrahamic religions to begin creating a bridge across their divides."*

Asking God to "pray," to "appear" on the soles of feet, to exert himself on our behalf, and later to "be still and listen" seems pushy and irreverent. The first time I read this series of poems, I almost laid them aside, but their candor, intimacy, and odd shifts of perspective tugged me back. The speaker is compelling, in more than one sense: these psalms dare us, as some of the biblical psalms do, to participate in prayer that refuses to soften the hard edges of faith. They reiterate the audacity and humility of the man who begged Jesus to heal his son, crying at the same time, "I believe; help my unbelief!" They confess doubt; they insist; they announce ongoing impatience with self-satisfied zealots and people who are all talk. Yet their impertinences throw into high relief a sturdy, rough-edged humility, an urgency, a hunger, not just for bread (though the speaker might well be an unhoused person whose belly is empty) but for a real, satisfying, meaty righteousness.

The images in the poems appear a little ad hoc, as though occurring to the speaker in the course of praying. Each line seems, in its way, a restart after a tentative and uncertain pause. After the one-word line "pray," for example, he seems to consider how: "aloud against the clamor of the human hand. . . ." Not the human mouth or voice, but the hand, which we have to imagine with instruments or tools or weapons of war—the noise of manufacture and technology and wanton destruction. Then, against that loudness comes the appeal to "appear on quiet soles." Then, later, to lead me, not exactly "in paths of righteousness," but "all the way to

* See http:www.bobcornwall.com.2013/10/99-psalms-said-review.html.

51

your bread"—a petition made boldly undiplomatic by raw need—
and all that way to "stay with me" and "be still."

The prayers are full of the self-interest of one who is hell-bent
on survival—spiritual as well as physical, as though the two are
inseparable. The speaker is aware that survival is a struggle—that
one's hold on it may be tenuous; that doubts assail and dread
threatens defeat; that we may, in the process, be devoured. In the
Narnia books that C. S. Lewis wrote for children, the lion Aslan
represents divine presence and protection, but is never predictable
or tame. When a child asks if Aslan is "safe," she receives this not
wholly reassuring reply: "Safe? . . . Who said anything about safe?
'Course he isn't safe. But he's good. He's the king, I tell you." The
lord who speaks from afar in the "unharried speech of animals/
who watch us from afar / with their unadulterated hunger" may,
like those animals, embody both power and innocence beyond
our understanding, and love that eludes human comprehension.

These prayers venture into the wild spaces where such Beings
dwell—unknown and unknowable beyond a scattering of facts
and centuries of speculation, yet able to be reached by whatever
words arise from the yearning of the human heart. This God, the
prayers attest, will not despise "a broken spirit, a broken and con-
trite heart." Nor, the speaker apparently believes, the tough and
troubled love learned on street corners and in depths of a despair
only God can plumb.

Marilyn McEntyre

Assurance

Pillars of light guide you,
and waves part.

Even by day the fire
that rises high in the night
blazes against the sun.

You will cross over
unafraid, and your way
will be safe.

Over every rushing stream
a bridge, and before you the presence
that shines in all that is.

Sometimes a prayer is a thing heard instead of spoken. Some-
times, when the mind is quieted and the heart open, the directives

we need, or the reminders, or the reassurances, come. In images or phrases or whole sentences—or, now and then, a poem—what we long for is given. I cherish these particular prayer experiences, and have learned not to over-think them: I may ask, as words come and shape themselves into lines, whether my inner hearing is faithful and accurate, but mostly I believe that when words come as gifts in times of prayer, the simplest and right response is gratitude.

That was how this poem came. I wrote it, as I have many others, in response to an artwork—an abstract print by Anthony Askew, an artist and man of faith whose rich visual imagination and sensibility have blessed me. Meaning, I have found, emerges from images, as from dreams, when I allow my gaze to linger, unhurried, and pay attention to what feelings and memories they awaken. Sometimes, I have also come to recognize, a work of visual art is an act of prayer, just as a poem may be.

This particular image, composed of layered vertical swaths of white, yellow, and rust bridged by brown, rope-like lines, seemed, as I gazed at it, to beckon me into encounter. It filled the eye with desert colors, suggesting the meeting of earth and sun, soil and light, and offering a stark reminder of the many biblical scenes of wrestling, fleeing, waiting, wandering, and meeting God, fearful and wonderful, in dry, sun-drenched, frightening places.

I found myself remembering the Israelites whose flight from Egypt was guided by a pillar of cloud by day and of fire by night, and of the Red Sea parting, and the first two lines of the poem suddenly came, not simply as a recollected fact or story, but as personal address. I realized how, in recent months, I had been guided, and a way had been opened through a thicket of complications.

As I wrestled with God, I found myself held fast in the protective embrace of my divine adversary, who was, and is, in fact, "a very present help in time of trouble."

I remembered, too, as I gazed at the brilliant whites so evocative of unveiled noonday sun, John's simple declaration that "God is light," and thought of the myriad ways light reaches us, enfolds us, exposes us, lights our way, and sometimes nearly blinds us.

I have always loved the phrase "light from light" in the Nicene Creed. Like "grace upon grace," it suggests a cascade, a lightfall of tumbling photons driven outward from the divine Source on a force like wind. We are showered in light, and behind the light we see there is the light we cannot see. When I was very young, I remember my mother explaining to me that the stars were still in the sky in the daytime, though we couldn't see them because the sunlight hid them. I was captivated by that fact. It seemed strange that light would hide what we could see in the darkness. Later, that same strangeness attached to the image of God as "robed in light." So, where the white I saw before me began to seem very like a pillar of fire, I imagined that fire not dying out by day, but hidden, like the stars.

These days I think a lot about guidance. I'm interested in how people receive guidance, recognize it, discern what is "of God" and what is more likely a simple matter of preference or inclination. I wonder about what we call intuition—being taught or instructed from within. I think about the ordinary language we put to moments of awakening or direction: "It occurred to me . . . ," "I found myself . . . ," "It came to me . . . ," "Something stopped me in my tracks . . . ," "I was led. . . ." We are led. Once I allow myself to recognize in my decisions an element of the unexpected, the nonrational, the surprisingly confident impulse to abandon the pro-and-con list, I begin to become aware of that "pillar of fire" that even in the day draws me toward its light.

That confidence came as the poem did, with an assurance against many odds: "You will cross over unafraid / and your way will be safe." There is much to be afraid of these days. I devote more attention to national and international news than may be good for me—to climate change and polluted oceans and warfare and other forms of terrorism. I think often of the angels' greeting: "Be not afraid." So when this line of the poem emerged, it took me by surprise. It was not an imperative or an admonition, but a promise: Whatever crossing you are facing, whatever barrier must be breached, you *will* be unafraid. When it is expressed this way, I begin to see that freedom from fear is not a state of mind to be mastered, but a gift of grace. I don't have to make myself unafraid. When the time comes, if I am open to grace, even when it looks, itself, a little threatening, I will be unafraid. In light of that promise, I am able to imagine that whatever it is that enables ordinary people to drag children from under truck wheels or stand in front of an assault rifle to protect students or face down wildfires to rescue trapped animals might also enable me, when the time comes, to face whatever I'm called to face. It is an assurance: What you need is near, and available.

The great classic adventure stories I have loved reinforce this archetypal theme: the weak whose hearts are open and willing will be made strong; the humble will be exalted; those who consent to the journey will learn by going where they have to go. My husband and I recently embarked once again on *The Fellowship of the Ring* with a grandson who hasn't yet made his way through that magnificent story. It's a tale that has richly reinforced and enhanced my awareness of how much happens by (as Aeschylus put it) "the awful grace of God," and moves in mysterious ways. When Gandalf appears, or Tom Bombadil, to assist the hobbits in times of danger, I remember stories of angels and guides who stopped travelers on the road or in the night and showed them a way they had not planned to go or infused them with a courage they would never have suspected in themselves. Over every rushing stream, they seemed to find a bridge.

To me, all sacred stories seem to point to this: that light shines in all that is. That divine Presence is omnipresent. That when we can see in every bush a burning bush, we will know what it is to pray without ceasing.

→ Praying ←

George Herbert

The Call

Come, my Way, my Truth, my Life:
Such a Way, as gives us breath:
Such a Truth, as ends all strife:
Such a Life, as killeth death.

Come, my Light, my Feast, my Strength:
Such a Light, as shows a feast:
Such a Feast, as mends in length:
Such a Strength, as makes his guest.

Come, my Joy, my Love, my Heart:
Such a Joy, as none can move:
Such a Love, as none can part:
Such a Heart, as joyes in love.

Anglicans have appropriated some very fine poems over the years
and made them into hymns. This lovely, lilting poem, originally

published in 1633, is one of them, written by one of the most devout and lyrical of the seventeenth-century English "metaphysical poets." As indicative as any I know of what purity of heart and desire for God look like, it moves seamlessly, as you read it, into song. The simple intimacy of the personal pronoun—"*my* Way, *my* Truth, *my* Life"—invites all who pray this prayer to take Christ's self-disclosure personally.

The imperative that starts each stanza, "Come," suggests an eagerness and an urgency and a depth of desire that accumulate in the course of the twelve deceptively simple lines. Imperatives have always seemed to me an uncomfortable form to introduce into prayer. We are told to ask for what we need, and some of the parables seem even to encourage us to ask again and again, to the point of being nuisances. But the Lord's Prayer in English, for all its list of petitions, at least begins in the polite subjunctive: "Thy will be done." It seems so much more respectful than "Do what you know needs to be done." By the time we get to "give us" and "forgive us" and "lead us not" and "deliver us," we've eased ourselves into God's company with a full acknowledgment of divine sovereignty that allows us to venture into more forthright demands.

Whether command or invitation, imperatives bring us into face-to-face encounter. They assume and urge action. The heartbeat of Herbert's poem, and the whole of its focus, lie in that one-word call: "Come." I'm reminded when I read it of a friend's moving public prayer that ended with words that appear in the final verses of Revelation—"Come, Lord Jesus." When I heard them in the context of a prayer otherwise focused on the needs of our community at the moment, on issues of personal, public, and institutional concern, they suddenly blew the frame and the moment open. Suddenly all of Christian history unrolled in that word,

"Come"—all the waiting and hoping and expecting and speculating and imagining when. And suddenly our collective desires seemed lifted out of daily concerns and refocused on the "desire of the everlasting hills." "Come" ranges from a prayer for awareness of God's presence in this moment, this day, this encounter, this task, to a prayer for the coming of a new heaven and a new earth, transformation of history, the fulfillment of eschatological hope.

That powerful petition is followed in each stanza by little gem-like meditations on who Christ is. The "way" that "gives us breath" is the One who was there from the foundation of the world, who breathed life into dust, whose creative work sustains us, and who, in our very genomes, has opened a path of development we even now can barely fathom.

The "truth" that "ends all strife" is the truth that will set us free. It is hard, in the midst of a thickening tangle of lies and spin and half-truths, to know how to find reliable information, to figure out who is trustworthy, to decide how to speak or hear a word of truth when language itself has been bent and hammered into an instrument of propaganda. How we "speak peace" in the midst of an economy largely dependent on war and a culture that valorizes violence is one of the great challenges of our time. To imagine, as Herbert does, a truth that "ends all strife" is to suggest that a mark of truth—God's truth—is that it will be a message and an agent of peace. Jesus's claim goes beyond an assurance that he speaks the truth: he *is* the truth—embodied, enacted, irreducible to maxim or law. And so, it seems, the way to peace lies in living truth, not in teachings or utterances alone.

The "life" that "killeth death" is a living force, summoned here not only as a reminder of an atoning sacrifice accomplished once for all, but also as divine energy, available when the human spirit flags, when faith weakens and hope wanes, and when, in despair, death looms like a dark lord. It is clear from some of Herbert's other poetry that he suffered those conditions on occasion, and that his petition is no idle recitation for the sake of poetic form and rhetorical effect, but a real and urgent call for help.

In a similar way, the "light" that "shows a feast" asks for restoration or renewal of a perspective on the human story that frames it in terms of hope for the heavenly banquet. Asking for that light, the speaker asks for a vision like the one given John on Patmos, perhaps, that will sustain hope and keep the sufferings of this world and this life in a perspective that makes them not only tolerable but meaningful.

The quaint and antique description of the "feast" that "mends in length" recalls that the heavenly banquet will be celebrated in an eternal now in an endless fullness that will make up for what so often seems the tragic brevity of life here. No matter how long earthly life is, it often seems too short when death comes; death always, I believe, leaves those remaining with a sense of incompletion. But the feast that awaits us, the speaker reminds himself, will mend what is torn at every graveside.

And at that banquet, the guests will be those who are not only invited, but re-created, resurrected, renewed, body and soul, for the occasion. Lifted up by "the strong hand of the Lord," we will be remade into God's guests, made ready, made welcome, made whole.

The "joy" that "none can move" and the "love" that "none can part" refer, we should remember, not only to what Christ imparts, but to who Christ is. Herbert's sacramental understanding of the emotions awakened in us by the lively, immediate, loving presence of the Spirit who is Christ's breath in us is, in its way, shocking. The joy and the love and, finally, the heart itself—the seat of all feeling, the place where life renews itself with every beat—are manifestations of God's own life in us.

God is already here. Christ has promised to be with us. The Holy Spirit dwells in and around us. Yet still, as we read this poem, we pray with the poet, "Come." More than a summoning of One who is already here, it is, perhaps, a prayer for awakening: Attune me. Make me more fully aware, receptive, responsive to your presence. Heart of my own heart, enliven in me a heart that "joyes in love."

The final line encompasses the rest. When love is our deepest joy, loving will be what we enact, what we embody, how we see. Love will inform our understanding and our motives. Imagine being "in love" in that way—dwelling in it, walking in it, seeing by it, moved to laughter and tears by it, letting love feed imagination and every encounter. Most of us don't live that way with any consistency. But Herbert's prayer gives me a little vision of what it might be like to find that lightness of being, that sure and lilting hope that turns words to song and imparts a bit of what it prays for—such a way and life and joy as to give us all the manna we need for the moment we're given.

Thomas Merton

The Candlemas Procession

Lumen
Ad revelationem gentium.

Look kindly, Jesus, where we come,
New Simeons, to kindle,
Each at Your infant sacrifice his own life's candle.

And when Your flame turns into many tongues,
See how the One is multiplied, among us, hundreds!
And goes among the humble, and consoles our sinful
    kindred.

It is for this we come,
And, kneeling, each receive one flame:
Ad revelationem gentium.

Our lives, like candles, spell this simple symbol:

Weep like our bodily life, sweet work of bees,
Sweeten the world, with your slow sacrifice.

And this shall be our praise:
That by our glad expense, our Father's will
Burned and consumed us for a parable.

Nor burn we now with brown and smoky flames, but bright
Until our sacrifice is done,
(By which not we, but You are known)
And then, returning to our Father, one by one,
Give back our lives like wise and waxen lights.

I can't think of a lovelier way of describing sacrifice made in faith
and obedience than "our glad expense." Sacrifice costs some-
thing—sometimes a great deal—but when it is willing, we are not
inclined to count. When we act in faith, we offer what we have,
gladly, to those we love, to God, to those in need whose claims on
us are clear and pressing and ever-present. We offer it, with God's
help, "in gladness and singleness of heart." Candles, as Merton
beautifully shows us here, are fit symbols of living sacrifice—of
life slowly turning matter to energy, time to light. In 1943, when
Merton, a contemplative and a Trappist monk, wrote this poem,
the many lives that were being sacrificed must have lurked in his
awareness as he turned his attention, and his readers', toward a
light that shone into deepening darkness.

We burn candles a lot in our home. I have come to love the
way, when a candle is lit before prayer and left burning, its burn-
ing extends the memory and intention of that prayer through its
hours of quietly lighting its corner of the room. When I meet with

my spiritual director, who lives three time zones away, we're using the electronic convenience of FaceTime, but I light a candle in my room and she in hers as we begin our reflections. Even in broad daylight, it helps me to have a candle burning as I write. The simple liturgical phrase "Light of Christ" comes to me often as I glance up and see it, steady and reassuring, reminding me of the real and quiet presence of the Spirit who guides and sustains. We burn them at each meal, including breakfast. We light them in the hours before bedtime where they bring the waning energies of the day into a centering stillness—or keep their quiet reminder nearby even when we're watching British mysteries on TV.

Candlemas is the traditional celebration of Jesus's presentation at the temple, an ancient ritual occasion marked by two prophetic utterances. One was Simeon's "*Nunc dimittis*": "Lord, now you are letting your servant depart in peace, according to your word; for my eyes have seen your salvation . . . a light for revelation to the Gentiles and for glory to your people Israel." Simeon follows his joyful recognition of Jesus as the promised one by a darker word to Mary: "and a sword will pierce through your own soul." A light is held against the darkness—a marvelous light that we still live by. And though darkness has not overcome it, darkness persists.

So we come to the altar, or to whatever place we are called on this feast day and on any ordinary day, to that light, trimming our wicks and seeking to be renewed by a gift that is never diminished. Whether or not we celebrate—or even recognize—Candlemas as a feast day, it is an idea and an image that elegantly signify what we are called to do as humans who seek to live by the light of Christ: be lit, burn quietly and steadily, letting ourselves slowly, gently be turned to light, "consumed for a parable," allowing our lives to be witnessed as examples of divine fidelity and our forgivenness and grateful transformation.

At the altar on Candlemas, the one flame "turns into many tongues," like those that burned over the disciples in the upper room, each worshiper carrying one back to whatever community he or she calls home. "Many tongues" is also a reminder of Pentecost and of how the one Word—the child who was the "word within a word, unable to speak a word"—became many and various—shouted and unshackled from ancient law, turned to a song of grace.

Merton's prayer begins with a petition that echoes throughout the poem: "Look kindly, Jesus, where we come...." See us. Witness our efforts. Watch for us as we make our way to you. Accept our intentions. Meet us where we kneel and strike light into our darkness. Let us be radiant with your light, "by which not we, but You are known." See us through.

Denise Levertov

The Avowal

As swimmers dare
to lie face to the sky
and water bears them,
as hawks rest upon air
and air sustains them,
so would I learn to attain
freefall, and float
into Creator Spirit's deep embrace,
knowing no effort earns
that all-surrounding grace.

I learned to float the way most children learn: my mother supported me in the water, her hands spread under my stiffened back, and I attempted, generally in vain, to relax. It's hard to believe water will hold you up. It's hard not to imagine that if you're released, you'll sink like a stone. But, after a certain amount of flailing and sputtering, it happened. Quietly, after my repeated requests not to let me go, she let me go, and the water bore me.

The first three lines of "The Avowal," a poem Levertov wrote shortly after her 1989 conversion to Catholicism, awaken that visceral memory—the edge of fear, the curiosity, the little flickers of daring, and the lasting lesson about full-bodied trust. Floating, as much as any early experience I remember, taught me about trust. Though I climbed a challenging tree now and then, and worked up some speed on my roller skates, I wasn't a particularly daring child. I'd try things, but it helped to have plentiful reassurance beforehand, and a back-up crew. So when the moment came to lie face to the sky and let the water bear me, I was exhilarated, and, somehow, my heart opened a little wider. Here was one more thing I could afford not to be anxious about. It was a moment of learning about faith.

It's not only trusting the water and the buoyancy of the body but facing the sky that makes that first experience of floating epiphanic. In the same way, I loved to lie in the grass, looking up at the sky, day or—when allowed—night. The vastness, the unimaginable distance of light years, the news that the visible starlight was old, from stars that might already have gone out—all these and the sense of my own incomprehensible smallness in the scheme of things brought me to the edge of mystery, or what one physicist called "radical amazement." Awe and fear are close neighbors. My brother, an amateur astronomer even at a tender age, used to recite facts that involved large numbers in powers of ten, assure me that there were meteors and meteorites on their way toward earth, and then drift off to sleep at night, leaving me to lie awake, wondering how to live with this unsettling information.

To lie face to the sky on water, I have learned, is to place oneself right at the riparian edge between heaven and earth, and discover how precarious and precious life on that edge is.

The poem makes no statement about that experience, except to let it hang, a suspended simile that continues to pique the reader's imagination while it turns to another image: hawks resting on air that sustains them. Hawks aren't altogether unusual where we live—not as rare a sight as eagles or condors or even red-winged blackbirds—but still arresting enough to make one pause and watch when they hover, scanning for prey, or fall in what poet Ted Olson unforgettably termed a "perilous, lovely way . . . down the long hill of wind. . . ." I imagine a lot of small muscles are involved even in that falling, and certainly in the way hawks "rest upon air." Like all good predators, they remain alert even in repose, and ready. But to see them high above us, going nowhere, knowing the wind the way an ocean swimmer knows the tide, the way a mole knows the soil or a singer the feel of middle C, is humbling and thrilling. The sight awakens a longing that's hard to name. I'd like to rest like that, in the very midst of things. I'd like to dare to do that.

Five lines into the poem, we have only introductory clauses. It is not yet a sentence, but hovers the way the images do, in no hurry to name the desire those images evoke. Then it comes: "So would I learn to attain / freefall and float / into Creator Spirit's deep embrace. . . ." I read the words for the first time with a shock of recognition. I have since seen that same look of sudden knowing on students' or friends' faces when I share the poem. "Yes," we say to ourselves or each other, "that's it." We want to trust like that. We want to let go of anxiety, hypervigilance, self-scrutiny, timidity, goals, and agendas and totally entrust ourselves.

Perhaps the most striking word in the poem is "attain." It drives right to the paradox every good coach knows—that the deep relaxation and readiness the best athletes achieve is hard-won, a product of rigorous training and sustained, self-correcting humility. Most of us don't learn to float easily, or to hang-glide (ever) or surf or dance on a stage or improvise a speech or act on a hunch we suspect is divine guidance. "Just relax into it," one coach told me, again and again. And I say it to students who hover, paralyzed, over keyboards and empty screens, dreading the first sentence. And then we work on relaxing.

And so I imagine that miraculous moment of floating "into Creator Spirit's deep embrace," not needing to know how deep I might go, not clinging to what I find hardest to let go. There are moments in prayer when you know you are held and loved, when words give way to wordlessness and Presence is utterly sufficient. They are precious. And they are—as Levertov reminds us in the final line, as she eases us onto solid doctrine—unearned, a pure gift of pure love poured out even upon those so slow and reluctant to trust, available as soon as we let go, even as we sputter, like the child in the pool, "Don't let go."

Galway Kinnell

Prayer

Whatever happens. Whatever
what is is is what
I want. Only that. But that.

"Whatever" has become a gesture of indecision, a casual conces-
sion offered when one doesn't have the interest or energy to be the
decider. Whatever you want. Whatever you all decide. Whatever.
Let's move on.

Reducing it to a dismissive wave, we forget what a wide and
hospitable word it can be. "Whatever you need, I'll be there." "I'm
in it for the long haul, whatever is required." Even when it bespeaks
a slightly delusional confidence that we can make so extravagant
a promise, "whatever" gives some measure of generous intention.
To begin a prayer with it, as Kinnell does in this poem written not
long before his death in 2014, is to restore its largeness: we recog-
nize in it an echo of "Thy will be done."

"Whatever happens." The period that abruptly makes those two words a sentence requires us to heft the full weight of the phrase. We hear wedding vows in it, and the impassioned promises of young love and vows of loyalty between friends. We hear "unto death" and "no matter what" and "the whole nine yards." A lot can happen. Sickness will come, or death will part us, and "poorer" may never become "richer." To declare that "whatever happens" is what I want is to fully, daringly, even brashly commit to radical contentment, taking no thought for the morrow, considering lilies and birds of the air, and accepting what you cannot change—"life on its own terms."

This prayer, written by an out-front activist, realist, and spiritually edgy poet of the Vietnam generation, is a little scary in a similar way to Father Thomas Keating's "Welcoming Prayer." Its bold affirmations always bring up, for me, flickers of self-doubt. I may *want* to welcome "all that comes to me today," including "all thoughts, feelings, emotions, persons, situations, and conditions," and to let go of my desire for power, control, affection, esteem, approval, pleasure, survival, and security, but am I really anywhere near actually welcoming them? I can put my heart into the final lines in which "I open myself to the presence of God and God's action within," but I'm left still wondering whether I actually have done all the welcoming and letting go required to give God room to act, "whatever happens."

Reading Kinnell's "Prayer" for the first time (and the second and third) made me smile. It still does. It reads like a riddle, or a haiku, or a koan, all of which deliver a surprise deftly, obliquely, eliciting laughter, puzzlement, and then reflection, then insight, sometimes dropping us suddenly, as off the end of a sandbar, into deep waters.

The words "whatever *what is* is is what I want" have to be parsed a second time before they make grammatical sense, and then pondered a while before they make rational sense. The sense they make may not, in fact, be rational. Because "what is" is apparently something of a mystery, at least to the speaker in this poem. He admits he's not sure what really is, and implies that we may be a little too hasty to assume we know what is. The visual and verbal playfulness of the sentence tricks us into recognizing that we don't know.

As I read it, I remember a TED talk by a physicist explaining how many dimensions (eleven, by his count, I believe) have been identified. I think of what physics has revealed about the paradoxical and often inscrutable character of *what is* at a subatomic level—about waves and particles and quantum leaps and neutrinos. And I think about how much of *what is* in the natural order we have endangered out of ignorant disregard. Ridding ourselves of inconvenient insects or bacteria, laying waste to rainforests and building developments in deserts, we disrupt *what is* (or at least what was and has been) in favor of what we want. I think of the large body of testimony to the existence of angels, near-death experiences, swift and dramatic answers to prayer—all a part of *what is* that defies full accounting. Whatever. I want that. I think.

It takes imagination and spiritual maturity to want what is—both what is given from the hand of God and what is strewn where heedless humans have passed. We get what we get. We are born and grow into it. To want it, though, is to calm vagrant desires, stop, and say yes without argument or further evidence. "Be joyful," Wendell Berry writes in one of his poems, "though you have considered all the facts." It may be that "be joyful" is another phrase for wanting *what is*.

"Only that." Nothing more, without impatience for change, willing to dwell with and in the moving stream of circumstances, welcoming them and not letting disordered desire drive wonder out. If we think we've somehow achieved a fine ethic of simplicity, that we don't want much, if we are among those who have read Thoreau or Lao-Tzu or the Gospel of Matthew and think we tread a little more lightly on the earth than our fellow pillagers, it's worth putting this attitude to the test: "only that." Try saying, for instance, "I want only the world I got, complete with its problems and threats." I want only to live where I live, in the body I got, with the car I have, the family and colleagues I have, the opportunities and limits my situation brings. I want the world as is, even as I do my part to heal its wounds and bring it peace.

Wanting only "what is" is not, I think, an opposition to working for change, but a basis for activism rooted in realism. Contentment drives out compulsive, distracting greed and challenges the narcissisms we have normalized. Wanting "only that" is not an end point, but a beginning.

And, significantly, the poem ends not only with an affirmation of contentment but of wanting. In the final, emphatic "But that," Kinnell insists on having life in full measure—as Thoreau did when he wrote that he wanted "not, when I came to die, [to] discover that I had not lived," and as Mary Oliver does when she writes that she wants not, when she comes to die, just "to have visited this world." One of Christopher Fry's most appealing characters in his delightfully dark 1948 play, *The Lady's Not for Burning*, set in the Middle Ages, is a woman being tried as a witch who very much wants to live. She affirms that same appetite for life in these memorable lines:

What is deep, as love is deep, I'll have
Deeply. What is good, as love is good,
I'll have well. Then if time and space
Have any purpose, I shall belong to it.

She lives in a dark age. The man she is coming to love finds the world, as Hamlet did, "weary, stale, flat, and unprofitable." But she wants that world, and will fight to stay in it as long as she can, because life is precious.

We might well wonder, when we see people in circumstances we pray to be spared, whether, in fact, life is precious on any terms. Kinnell's prayer presupposes that: Whatever is, I want that. Because whatever is, is mine to learn from, an occasion for trust or love or endurance or hope.

In each of its three lines the poem allows us flickers of amusement. It is playful in the way spiritual teachers are often playful. "Whatever happens. Whatever" teases us into curiosity and puts feeling first before making meaning. A second palindrome, *"what is* is is what" dares us again to read forward and backward and then forward again, reminding us that meaning is multidimensional and multidirectional, epiphanic and delightful even as it challenges us to confront hard things. The final line, though it continues a sentence already begun, also stands as its own statement of purpose: "I want. Only that. But that." It speaks with authority. It presumes a God who honors the claim of the heart's deepest desire—One who can promise in confidence (and did) that what we most truly desire, when we have learned to desire truly, will be granted because the desire itself will be of God.

Scott Cairns

Possible Answers to Prayer

Your petitions—though they continue to bear
just the one signature—have been duly recorded.
Your anxieties—despite their constant,

relatively narrow scope and inadvertent
entertainment value—nonetheless serve
to bring your person vividly to mind.

Your repentance—all but obscured beneath
a burgeoning, yellow fog of frankly more
conspicuous resentment—is sufficient.

Your intermittent concern for the sick,
the suffering, the needy poor is sometimes
recognizable to me, if not to them.

Your angers, your zeal, your lipsmackingly
righteous indignation toward the many
whose habits and sympathies offend you—

these must burn away before you'll apprehend
how near I am, with what fervor I adore
precisely these, the several who rouse your passions.

It is possible to pray badly. When the disciples ask Jesus, "Teach us to pray," they seem to be aware that prayer involves practice—even a learning curve—and some serious retraining in habits of the heart. "Possible Answers to Prayer," which Cairns, an Orthodox poet, published in 2002, offers a wry, timely look at a few of the varieties of self-deception that those who pray are prey to. (Forgive the pun—or muse upon it—as you wish.) These delusions are common among pious folk and are identified here by a compassionate God persona whose response to the misguided prayers of his wayward flock is a little like Jesus's response to a disciple's moments of cluelessness: "Have I been with you so long, Philip, and still you do not know me?"

The God-speaker in the poem begins by commenting on petitions that "bear just the one signature"—prayers for purely personal concerns that focus narrowly on those to the evident exclusion of the broader implications, social contexts, and consequences for others of what one prays for. Even these, some of which might rightly be recognized as drivel, are "duly recorded." They are heard and remembered. They are, more often than we deserve, generously answered. But they underestimate and underutilize the power of prayer to widen the heart and the scope of compassion by connecting one's own immediate needs with those of the world. These are the prayers that C. S. Lewis may have in mind when he writes in his 1942 sermon "Weight of glory, "

It would seem that Our Lord finds our desires not too strong, but too weak. We are half-hearted creatures, fooling about with drink and sex and ambition when infinite joy is offered us, like an ignorant child who wants to go on making mud pies in a slum because he cannot imagine what is meant by the offer of a holiday at the sea. We are far too easily pleased.

Just as a holiday at the sea widens the eye and deepens the breath, so the scope and power of prayer may achieve greater things when the one who prays begins to connect private with public concerns—the personal with the political, one's own desires with others' needs. As I pray for my children and grandchildren, I can learn to widen the nets and lift up others' children, and all the children in a rising generation that is facing a world with new and unprecedented problems. In this way, legitimate but unimaginative and self-focused petitions may grow into broad visions of hope and energy directed toward needed healing and transformation.

The anxieties we bring before the throne of grace likewise often reflect our insularity and our imperviousness to the divine messages, delivered again and again in Scripture and story: "Be not afraid." "Be anxious about nothing." "Peace be with you." The God who speaks in this poem hears the petitioner's anxious pleas with tolerance and even amusement, knowing how needless are the nervous ditherings of a child being held safely in a thunderstorm. The anxieties barely need attention, but the anxious person does, and receives it despite persisting in such "little faith."

And as God accepts anxious prayers where trust would be so much better, so he also accepts as "sufficient" even grudging repentance still polluted with lingering resentments. I think here of how hard it is to pray open-heartedly for leaders who abuse power and privilege, or for those I think have hurt me, and how easily the poison of self-righteousness seeps into those prayers. To repent of that self-righteousness is also hard without some of it tainting contrition with a residue of contempt.

Even prayer for the needy without the almsgiving that would put it into action is received at the throne of limitless grace, despite James's fair warning that "faith without works is dead." Nowhere is the disconnection between faith and works clearer, perhaps, than in those prayers we lift up every day at mealtime that we remain "mindful of the needs of others" before we turn to our own abundant meal of organic foods we can afford to buy from the local farmers' market. The speaker's observation that the sick and suffering would barely recognize our concern in the rote intercessions softens quickly into an assurance that God accepts even our slight attempts, our small, perfunctory gestures of compassion, willing to wait for our slow learning and, in the meantime, supplement our deficiencies.

But the poem ends with a warning: all our unjust judgments, our self-satisfactions, self-exonerations, self-justifications, must "burn away" before we can begin to "apprehend" the love of God that searches out not only us and our kind, but the whole struggling, sorry, stumbling lot of humankind on this earthly journey. It is a love, as one hymn puts it, that is "broader than the measures of the mind"—certainly broader than most of our minds, confined as they are to particular political, theological, and social bandwidths, hemmed in by the limits of custom and conditioning.

Each triad in this amusing, convicting poem offers both accusation and assurance, and offers a little glimpse of how judgment and mercy co-exist. As we have learned, if we've been listening, God passes no judgment without mercy, and offers no mercy without judgment. In the spirit of O'Connor's preacher who insists that "God's mercy burns!," we realize that it does, but the adverb matters: it "burns away" what has to be cleared for new growth to happen. "Teach us to pray" is a prayer that takes courage: it invites God's scrutiny, judgment, correction, redirection. It subjects dearly held habits to change. But we can, I think, trust that strenuous and sometimes painful growth in faith and wisdom takes place in safe and secure relationship to a God who loves us so much that he can afford to laugh.

Mary Oliver

Praying

It doesn't have to be
the blue iris, it could be
weeds in a vacant lot, or a few
small stones; just
pay attention, then patch
a few words together and don't try
to make them elaborate, this isn't
a contest but the doorway
into thanks, and a silence in which
another voice may speak.

"Praying" isn't exactly a prayer, though the title, artfully ambiguous, suggests that pausing to reflect on praying is itself an act of praying. The poem reminds me of how prayer overlaps with one's own interior monologue—the "self-talk" that includes hopeful affirmations, recitations of what one knows and needs to reclaim, words from the inner teacher who occasionally alerts us to what we didn't know we knew. Sometimes we pull words out of deep memory banks, where we store them for moments of need. Sometimes they come from elsewhere—from the Spirit who guides us and addresses us in ways few of us have learned fully to acknowledge.

These words come from a collection published during a period of great personal loss for the poet. They seem, in that context, to extend comfort: grief brings exhaustion; it is hard to pray one's way through the dailiness of sorrow. But prayer is a gentle task, and may, if we keep it mercifully simple, heal our hearts almost effortlessly.

The opening phrase, "It doesn't have to be . . . ," introduces the business of praying in terms of permission. Longtime readers of Oliver's poetry will recognize in it an echo of the opening line of her poem "Wild Geese": "You do not have to be good." The words release us from imperatives and moralistic constraints that may be impeding the very freedom required to enter into a state of grace and a dialogue with the Divine Listener.

Anything—weeds, small stones—can occasion that grace. Though the blue iris may move us with its delicacy, the depth of its color, or a symmetry and complexity of form we have learned to call beautiful, prayerful awareness doesn't depend on beauty—at least not on beauty defined by aesthetic conventions. Good photographers know how often a weed or a stone might become a key element in a composition that surprises the eye and mind into a sudden apprehension of radiance in what might ordinarily be overlooked. Openness to such incidental beauty, sudden reframings that transform the ordinary and even the "ugly," is a matter of both willingness and practice.

The practice of noticing opens the heart to gratitude and leads, at least for this poet and for many who pray, to an impulse to address the Source of what has been seen. So we "patch a few words together," words sometimes spontaneous, sometimes learned by heart and carried there for ready use when the heart is turned to prayer. Either is sufficient.

While visiting a 98-year-old hospice patient, I was moved to learn that he had recited every night since the age of six the simple German prayer his mother had taught him. He was a highly educated professional, a man of some sophistication and broad interests and tastes. But the childhood prayer—really just a few simple words patched together for a child's sleepy recitation—still served him in a way that was not simply sentimental. After reciting it for me, he told me how it had kept him in touch with Jesus through many hard times when he might have been driven away from God altogether.

He was grateful. And he had nothing to prove. That prayer— along, doubtless, with others he devised and discovered in adult life—kept a doorway open that led him to the thanks he readily expressed and perhaps also, even on his last night, into the silence where he could hear God's voice.

The line breaks in "Praying" reinforce its message—a strong corrective to the harmful anxieties that make prayer an unsettling or unappealing venture. Immediately following the permission given in "It doesn't have to be," we are offered possibility: "it could be." And only "a few" will suffice: pausing on "a few," we're invited to recognize that whatever it is that occasions the prayer of the heart, it doesn't take much to move from observation to encounter. My favorite line break comes after "don't try." It's hard not to try—to open and allow rather than making the effort that leads, after all, to scrupulosity and spiritual pride or frustration. Prayers, even the most elegant, begin here—in receiving, allowing, humbling, patching, entering into a place that has been provided, and listening.

Marin Sorescu

Prayer

Translated by Gabriela Dragnea

Oh you saints,
Let me enter your society,
If only as a statistician.

You're old,
Perhaps the years are
Getting you down by now,
Laying themselves over you
In layers of color.

Just let me take care
Of your dirty work in
All the nooks and crannies.

For example I could
Swallow light
At the Last Supper
And exhale your halos
After the devotionals.

From time to time,
At a distance of half a wall,
I could
Form my hands into a horn
And shout,
Now for the believers,
Now for the unbelievers
Hallelujah! Hallelujah!

Whimsical as it is, something in this piquant appeal to the saints touches my heart. I recognize in it the very human, childlike desire just to "hang around" with the people one admires, watch them, learn from them, enjoy their company. Any of us who spent certain school years on the margins of a particular in-group, not quite a member, though not entirely excluded, may remember the feeling of wanting to be accepted, but also of not being quite ready to be "one of them."

The analogy occurs to me as I reread this 1991 poem by Sorescu, a courageous Romanian poet and playwright. The speaker, evidently gazing at a painting, imagines entering into the company of the saints, if only as a servant. He imagines what he might do for them and among them. He could be "a statistician," perhaps documenting their miracles, keeping a census of their growing numbers, counting the churches, schools, and hospitals established in their names. He could hold their halos like hats, carrying their light in his own lungs, breathing it back to them in due time. He could be a kind of mascot or runner, a water boy, a cheerleader who sends up the shout to be echoed by millions, starting a wave of rejoicing with his own "Hallelujah!"

I am reminded, in these eager imaginings, of walking down the long aisle of Our Lady of the Angels, the Catholic cathedral in Los Angeles. Tapestries lining both walls are filled with images of saints, named and unnamed, representing many generations, many peoples, many stories told and told again. All of them stand in profile, facing the altar—visible reminders to contemporary worshipers to pause a little longer over these words in the Creed: "I believe in . . . the communion of saints. . . ." On any given Sunday, the faithful who have gathered there stand among them—Mary Magdalene, St. Joseph, St. Francis, St. Catherine, martyrs, teachers, healers, slaves. I stood among them alone that day, imagining, like Sorescu's speaker, the questions I might ask them, imagining meeting them on another plane, finding my way into conversations that would lift me into a realm of divine intelligence and loving-kindness from which the pollutions of petty resentments, distractions, half-truths, and adulterated motives had been filtered, leaving only air and light and laughter like music.

I didn't grow up praying to saints. Even the term "saints" was used cautiously in my home. A conversation with a kindly priest in my early years helped open me up to the notion that we might address those who have gone before us in the long lineage of believers as friends and fellow travelers, seeking their help, recognizing them as our elders whose wisdom might serve us now.

The saints we name and remember from Christian history as particular models of faithful living are worth "hanging around." It's worth reading their stories—not, perhaps, the sanitized hagiographies, but the well-researched biographies that allow us to see some of the warp and woof, the tensions and stresses and struggles and surprises of lives informed by faith. It was from Catholic friends who were quite comfortable with prayer to saints, and with their membership in that wide communion, that I first learned this energetic hymn, which has also found its way into Protestant hymnals: "I sing a song of the saints of God, patient and brave and true. . . ." The verses catalog them: "one was a doctor, one was a queen, one was a shepherdess on the green . . . and one was a soldier and one was a priest and one was slain by a fierce wild beast. . . ." Each verse ends with the intention and the prayer that, "God helping," I might be one too. It's not too much to ask, in hope and delighted anticipation, believing that "there is no competition in the kingdom of heaven," where even "'the least' will be full of light" and gladness.

~❧ Witnessing ❧~

T. S. Eliot

From "The Dry Salvages"

IV
Lady, whose shrine stands on the promontory,
Pray for all those who are in ships, those
Whose business has to do with fish, and
Those concerned with every lawful traffic
And those who conduct them.

Repeat a prayer also on behalf of
Women who have seen their sons or husbands
Setting forth, and not returning:
Figlia del tuo figlio,
Queen of Heaven.

Also pray for those who were in ships, and
Ended their voyage on the sand, in the sea's lips
Or in the dark throat which will not reject them
Or wherever cannot reach them the sound of the sea bell's
Perpetual angelus.

When I began to consider writing a book about prayer poems, T. S. Eliot's *Four Quartets* were among the first that came to mind. Lyrical, mystical, and richly, deeply poetic, these poems, which Eliot wrote in London during a terrifying war with Germany—have inspired admiration and gratitude in generations of readers who have placed them among the great landmarks of Christian poetry and found in them a hospitable place for theological reflection and an invitation and incitement to prayer. They are, I believe, a record of a soul's journey and the fruit of extended meditation on the ways that divine Love infuses time, history, and the circumstances of a single human life. But, except for this short canto from *The Dry Salvages*, the third of the four poems that make up the *Quartets*, they are written not as prayer but rather as interior reflection in which the speaker is in a contemplative state.

This canto, though, a prayer addressed to Mary as Queen of Heaven, has a distinct Anglo-Catholic liturgical character. Like many of the prayers for particular people, groups, or occasions in the Book of Common Prayer, it focuses specifically but inclusively on "all" who are concerned with life on water—those who support them, those who await them at home, those who have died at sea.

The prayer, the fourth of five cantos, introduces a distinct change in rhythm and tone from the previous three, which represent a musing dramatic monologue—philosophical, speculative, thoughtful—uttered in the voice of a speaker who wonders and seeks and occasionally prophesies. Here, the speaker prays directly to the Queen of Heaven, asking for her intercession on behalf of all seafarers and those who await them. In the wide context of all the quartets, this brief prayer of petition stands out as a humble return to the forms prescribed by the church—received rather than invented, simply recited rather than elaborated. But it also assumes a metaphorical dimension: all of us are voyagers, faring forward, awaited or awaiting, facing down danger or loss.

And all of us are involved in the lives of those fellow voyagers for whom we pray. Brief as it is, this is an encompassing prayer: "all those" for whom the speaker prays include whole classes of people for whom, as the old Book of Common Prayer says, it is our "bounden duty" to pray. We inherit forms like this one that teach us and keep us from mere self-interest or tribal loyalties. We are instructed to pray for "all in authority," "all those" who confess God's name, "all those who are in any way afflicted or distressed, in mind, body, or estate." These prayers are not simply sweeping abstractions that "cover the bases" and dispense with that bounden duty in one fell swoop, but strong verbal acts of solidarity—sometimes including people for whom we'd much rather not pray. We're all in it together. We are, as Paul put it, members of each other, and members also of distinct communities, professional guilds, circles of people bound by common circumstance. We are bound by common needs and linked by ties that bind.

That Mary is the one to whom the prayer is addressed links this prayer with those of Dante—a literary and spiritual ancestor to whom Eliot made frequent reference throughout his long career. But, more importantly, it links us to Mary, a humble and astonished human being who was chosen for a momentous, daunting mission, and, young and poor as she was, said yes. Protestants like those I grew up with have a strong resistance to the Catholic practice of praying to Mary or any other intercessor but Christ, but I have come to appreciate the value of addressing the wide communion of saints (among whom she does occupy a unique place) as brothers and sisters, gone before us on this journey, and available to intercede from that wide and mysterious realm where we hope one day to join them.

The Latin title for Mary that the poet includes here, *"Figlia del tuo figlio,"* "Daughter of your son," points to the great paradox of the Incarnation—that the Creator of the Universe came to us vulnerable and small, committed to the protection of a human being, and comes to us still in the poor and vulnerable, almighty and too often unnoticed.

Richard Wilbur

From "The Eye"

II

Preserve us, Lucy,
From the eye's nonsense, you by whom
Benighted Dante was beheld,
To whom he was beholden.

If the salesman's head
Rolls on the seat-back of the 'bus
In ugly sleep, his open mouth
Banjo-strung with spittle,

Forbid my vision
To take itself for a curious angel.
Remind me that I am here in body,
A passenger, and rumpled.

Charge me to see
In all bodies the beat of spirit,
Not merely in the tout en l'air
Or double pike with layout

But in the strong,
Shouldering gait of the legless man,
The calm walk of the blind young woman
Whose cane touches the curbstone

Correct my view
That the far mountain is much diminished,
That the fovea is prime composer,
That the lid's closure frees me.

Let me be touched
By the alien hands of love forever,
That this eye not be folly's loophole
But giver of due regard.

I happen to be writing this paragraph on a bus where I am, in fact, "a passenger, and rumpled," having risen at four A.M. to be shuttled through a TSA check and scanned (randomly) for sequestered knives, flown two thousand miles, and funneled toward ground transportation. As I look around at fellow passengers, I think about Wilbur's prayer, slightly abashed at how accurately it reflects my own need for correction. Several across the aisle are fingering their phones. One is looking out the window. She appears preoccupied and wistful. It's impossible not to wonder what demanding conversation she has just left behind, or is facing. So I make up stories about them, not all entirely compassionate. I have chosen to sit at the very back where there is more legroom but where, also, it is easier to "take my vision for a curious angel," to play reporter or spy, among, but not of, this quiet assembly gathered for an hour on a highway outside Chicago.

This prayer by poet laureate Wilbur is the second half of a 1976 poem that begins with a longish musing about a morning when the speaker idly watched, through borrowed binoculars, the activities of unsuspecting strangers on a neighboring terrace. Taken aback at his own slightly prurient curiosity, he wonders what "kept me goggling all that hour"—what was he hoping for? "Lewd espials?" or a moment of fine aesthetic pleasure in seeing what an "almond leaf became /within the sudden premise of a frame"?

Conscious of something more than a breach of propriety, the speaker turns his guilty musings into this remarkable prayer to St. Lucy, the figure in Dante's *Paradiso* who "did not abuse her eyesight for the sake of evil."* It begins as a general petition that *we* be preserved—we with eyes to see? We who hope to see with eyes of faith and compassion?—"from the eye's nonsense." One might stop right there and inscribe the sentence wherever one records prayers for life's occasions. How pervasively we are afflicted by the eye's nonsense as we stare at screens and thumb through tabloids at doctors' offices and peer at others' odd behavior in parks and on beaches.

A PBS series some years ago focused on our media-saturated environment—particularly on the barrage of larger-than-life and mass-produced images we face each day, especially if we live, as more and more of us do, in cities. Young children are routinely exposed to images of violence and indiscriminate sexuality. The poor are surrounded by occasions for crushing envy in ubiquitous depic-

* See http://taylormarshall.com/2012/12/saint-lucy-in-dantes-inferno-and.html.

tions of casual affluence. And we learn to gaze at two-dimensional animations rather than meeting the gaze of the truly animated beings who stand with us in long lines or sit beside us in a pew.

By the second stanza, though, the prayer takes a more personal turn. The speaker, troubled by his voyeuristic tendencies, recalls how he sees those he encounters in the course of an ordinary day—how he sees and judges what is unappealing or unsettling. The sleeping salesman, open-mouthed, the legless man, and the blind young woman represent so many from whom even the more compassionate among us might momentarily recoil or turn away, unsure whether we're exercising diplomacy or self-protection.

Susan Schweik, a leader in disability studies, has documented the dismaying history of the so-called ugly laws, ordinances that made "exposure" of "unsightly" bodies or embarrassing public behaviors associated with mental illness punishable. Horrifying as such laws seem, they testify to attitudes that continue to make the lives of people with visible disabilities harder. We tend, unless we consciously resist the inclination, to avert our gaze from the homeless person on the sidewalk who is also dirty and muttering invective. Or from the person in the wheelchair because it's "impolite to stare." Or sometimes we shudder in self-serving gratitude when we see someone severely disabled or injured because we wouldn't want to be them, or hurry our children past, praying catastrophe will never leave them disabled or disfigured. Most of us, assuming we are among those who enjoy the privilege of healthy, able bodies, find ways to overcome such unworthy feelings and self-correct. But it's good to check in with ourselves periodically about how we're seeing what we see— how judgment, fear, anxiety, or moral insularity affect our gaze.

Another petition the poem offers that is worth praying in its own right is the bold request for a deeper, subtler way of seeing:

"Charge me to see in all bodies / the beat of spirit. . . ." Not merely in the dancers and athletes, the Olympic skaters and the exquisite children on the playground, not merely in the beloved, but in the unlovely. To see like this demands a reorientation of the will that so easily veers toward self-satisfaction and self-focus. It requires a second or third look, a gaze sustained long enough to notice what dignity or patience or wit or justified indignation another may embody. To see others in terms of their stories, which we may never know, but may benefit from imagining.

Then come the more arresting petitions: that we remember that what we see is not the way things are—that the human eye is a limited instrument and the human perspective confined to a small bandwidth; and that we not kid ourselves that if we don't see it, it isn't there. That last may seem a laughable self-deception because it recalls small children who cover their eyes, thinking either they will disappear or we will. But the temptation to do exactly that is strong and pervasive in adult lives where much of the world's brokenness is so visible and overwhelming. The desire just not to know about horrors we can't help makes some sense; it isn't entirely culpable to preserve sanity by shielding ourselves from chronic anguish or the ache of costly compassion. So we may need to pray to be willing to look, and see, and perhaps weep, and gather and act.

The final stanza is, again, a single petition and a prayer complete in itself that's worth praying. To ask to be touched by love's "alien hands" is to recognize how love calls us out of the familiar and the comfortable and may lead us into strange encounters that disturb our peace. It is to pray that we not, finally, be counted among those who have eyes and see not, but among those willing to look on tempests or twisted lives or others' sorrow or, indeed, their success, giving all of them "due regard." The final phrase calls our attention to the social contract revised and sealed in the Gospels, where love of neighbor, as Jesus assured the disciples, may cost us not less than everything.

Each of the short, four-line stanzas in this poem directs both will and imagination with power and economy toward whatever has hovered at the periphery, waiting to be witnessed or discovered by someone willing to put down the binoculars and venture out and seek today's answer to the consequential question, "Who is my neighbor?"

Francisco X. Alarcón

L.A. Prayer

April 1992

something
was wrong
when buses
didn't come

streets
were no longer
streets

how easy
hands
became
weapons

blows
gunfire
rupturing
the night

the more
we run
the more
we burn

o god
show us
the way
lead us

spare us
from ever
turning into
walking

matches
amidst
so much
gasoline

Prayers erupt in moments of raw terror or fury—first comes the visceral reaction to danger or horror, and then, often before much thought intervenes, a prayer rises deep in the belly to drown the waking beast of fear. Francisco Alarcón, Mexican-American poet, educator, and, during his formative years, migrant farm worker, knew both fear and fury. His "L.A. Prayer," written in the wake of the "Rodney King riots" that erupted after a widely publicized incident of police brutality, traces the course of this kind of prayer in one- and two-word lines—bursts that might be spoken on the run. Not until the sixth breathless stanza is God invoked. The first five record an escalating awareness of danger—traffic flow paralyzed, streets transformed into battle zones and neighbors into armed adversaries. As all efforts to escape violence seem only to fuel it, the speaker finally utters cries familiar to every desperate human who has seen the depths: show us . . . lead us . . . spare us.

But then the final seven lines turn a prayer of abject need into something larger: the speaker prays not just that he and those he cares about be spared injury, dispossession, or death, not simply for a way out of the riots—a back road to safety—but for the largeness of spirit that might enable him to resist the lure of violence and the temptation to retaliate. He prays that he and others might not add fuel to the fires of hatred. In the midst of justifiable rage over what the Rodney King beatings, like other abuses of power, revealed about a system of privilege riddled with injustice, his prayer is not to make it worse.

Anna Deavere Smith's memorable one-woman stage play, *Twilight: Los Angeles, 1992*, depicts the responses of forty real-life eyewitnesses to the same riots. Having interviewed each of them extensively about their experiences of the riots, she plays each of them, male and female, young and old—a Korean grocer, a nameless juror in the King trial, the chief of police, a truck driver, and a congresswoman. Later filmed by PBS, the play has continued to generate necessary conversation about the deep roots of racism in L.A. and other American cities. It shows how people of every class and ethnicity live with the consequences of gang warfare, abuses of power, protection of privilege, exploitation of immigrants, and cycles of fear and hatred that play out on the streets. In the midst of it all, there are voices of compassion, wisdom, and understanding, all of them representing the survival of desire for reconciliation that runs even deeper than the currents of hate. Deavere Smith comments on her own work, which included long and difficult conversations about core conflicts: "Theater and film can participate in civic discourse and even influence national attitudes by using the power of entertainment, spectacle, and dialogue. At a time when our national conversation about race has become, to some extent, merely fragments of monologues, *Twilight: Los Angeles* seeks to create a conversation from these fragments."*

As urban violence has continued to erupt and a litany of names has been added to the long list of those who have suffered and died from police brutality or urban warfare, other artists have held up lenses and mirrors to help us see what's happening among us, and to invite us to respond. Alarcón's poem invites us to pray and shows us how. Prayer begins in noticing. The first stanza replicates stages of awakening to ambient danger, starting with simply "something." The word by itself is like a lift of the head, a sniff of the air, an intuitive response to a disturbance in the field. The second line drops the other shoe: "was wrong." Something was wrong. The speaker didn't know what yet, but recalls the feeling of unease. And what was it? The buses. Where were the buses? They didn't come.

Then the lens widens. To miss the buses is to notice whole streets filled with a swelling mob of angry people. "No longer streets" deftly identifies that liminal pause between not knowing and knowing—noticing, but not yet recognizing what's actually happening, because it doesn't register all at once. Then the partic-

* See https://www.gvsu.edu/theatre/twilight-los-angeles-1992-162.htm.

ulars: the hands that have become "weapons." When I read these lines, I think of how medical students have said that in their first experience of working on cadavers, the hardest part can be the hands. Hands that have done so many human things cannot simply be reduced to objects of study. Here, the hands-become-weapons signify a tragic transformation of people into bodies, commodities, cheap labor, threats.

The blows and gunfire "rupturing the night" remind us of the speaker's still-shocked point of view. In the original Latin, "rupture" was essentially a medical word that referred to the fracturing of limbs or other body parts, like ruptured hernias. That bit of etymological background adds a dimension to this line: what the speaker is witnessing isn't just civil disturbance or nighttime noise, but human brokenness.

Then a moment of reflection comes—a step back from the fray to recognize a larger truth: "the more / we run / the more / we burn." It's hard not to remember, as one reads those words, horrifying images of burning bodies running from houses or a child in flames on a road in Viet Nam. The flight instinct fails to serve survival. Running fans the flames.

Then comes the prayer. "O God" is a phrase so trivialized now in common speech that it comes as a slight surprise when we hear it echoing from the cliff edge of real desperation. It is both plea and demand: "Hear me!" "Where are you?" "O God, come to my aid." That it is a prayer for the whole community again widens the speaker's and the reader's consciousness to a perspective from which it becomes clear that we are all implicated and complicit. We all need to be shown the way, led through the dark night. And we all need what finally the poet prays for—to be spared a fate worse than physical harm. We need not to become the perpetrators, not to be turned into agents of hatred. We need to be people who can navigate all that volatility without inciting the hatred we fear.

The more I read this poem, the more I recognize how powerfully it reminds me what it costs to be a "peacemaker." I imagine walking through minefields, wading through spilled oil or gasoline, knowing how little it would take to set off a holocaust, daring to be there and not set off one spark. A mentor of mine once advised me on a strategy for dealing with someone else's fury: "Just try standing there, being a quiet presence, knowing who you are and what you're about. Don't react out of your own anxiety." To pray for peace is to pray for the courage to show up and bring peace to where there is no peace—to streets that are "no longer streets" where fists are raised and windows are shattered. It's not an invitation to take lightly. It is, when we find ourselves standing in those streets, a calling.

Anna Kamienska

Those Who Carry

Translated from the Polish by David Curzon and Grażyna Drabik

Those who carry grand pianos
to the tenth floor   wardrobes and coffins
the old man with a bundle of wood hobbling beyond the
    horizon
the woman with a hump of nettles
the lunatic pushing her baby carriage
full of empty vodka bottles
they all will be raised up
like a seagull feather   like a dry leaf
like eggshell   scraps of street newspapers

Blessed are those who carry
for they will be raised

My favorite lines in *Fiddler on the Roof* are the question Motel the
tailor asks the rabbi upon receiving a longed-for sewing machine,
and the rabbi's response:

"Rabbi, is there a blessing for a sewing machine?"
"There is a blessing for everything."

Blessing is a liturgical act, a spoken prayer—usually in the mysterious subjunctive—and also a way of seeing and responding that imparts as it witnesses. It is an attitude, like the "quality of mercy," which "blesseth him that gives and him that takes."

Anna Kamienska's blessing for "those who carry" draws a wide frame around a class of people we might not think to "lift up" for reverent attention or to see in terms of the hope we share with them rather than in terms, less generous, of mere pity. The lively, surprising specificity with which the speaker recognizes their efforts and their burdens, and compares them to other stray and ragged things that are "rasied up" invites us to pause over each with an admiration we might not otherwise feel. Kamienska, a Polish Catholic, knew the lives of burdened people: growing up in Nazi-occupied Poland, she taught in underground schools, wrote and watched and commemorated those whose fates could only be imagined. Appreciation requires imagination—a particular gift Kamienska brings to her work, written in the thick of World War II and in its long aftermath.

"Those who carry grand pianos," for instance, brings to my mind the huge, sweating, muscular young man who strapped our piano to his back and carried it down two flights of hillside steps to our door. He worked for a moving company staffed and supported by a thriving program for people recovering from addiction. Adhering to their rules, he accepted no tips—only a glass of cold water for his efforts. He was cheerful. That his unusual strength equipped him for service seemed to give him great satisfaction. He spoke with candor about rehab and with gratitude about having a job. He blessed us with more than a safely ensconced piano that day. That was some years ago, and until I read this poem, I'd had little occasion to remember him. Remembering him is a reminder of what recovery requires, and of how many are quietly walking that hard road a day at a time.

Those who carry coffins also walk a hard road—short and ceremonial, but paved with sorrow. They're usually the hardy sons or grandsons of the deceased—or nephews or devoted former students returned to pay respects. They are among the living whose health and strength seem almost jarring so closely adjacent to the dead. The physical weight of the coffin and the body of someone known and loved, hugged and held, whose familiar hands lie crossed and still, add a palpable dimension to loss and make the pallbearers representatives for the rest of us who watch them make their slow way along the route of the final journey. For some young people, it's a defining moment as they age into awareness of mortality.

Older people who have lived with that deepening awareness for many years may bear their daily burdens in intimate proximity to death. Like "the old man with a bundle of wood hobbling beyond the horizon," those who know the ache of aging bodies also know that they make a challenge of what might once have been simply and thoughtlessly accomplished. And the old woman carrying nettles for tea or medicine has gathered them, no doubt, at some cost to the modest reserve of daily energy required for survival. To see what they carry and to bless them as they go is to cultivate a solidarity that keeps us humanely aware that our times are in God's hands and that we are called, like Shakespeare's Gloucester, to endure our "going hence even as our coming hither."

Even "the lunatic pushing her baby carriage / full of empty vodka bottles" offers, and deserves, blessing. The neediest, the most helpless, the most lost among us offer outward and visible signs of all our brokenness, reminders to keep our hearts open rather than recoil—to engage the homeless person on the street corner, or the one who suffers from mental illness, in a simple exchange, to ask him or her a question, to look past an alcoholic haze to a chronic pain, aching and unassuaged, that deserves and calls forth blessing.

The list of "those who carry" is small and unassuming in this poem, which models the humility of which it speaks. But in it we're reminded to see those around us in terms of what they carry—what's borne in aging bodies and troubled minds and aching hearts—and to see ourselves in them.

"They will be raised," the speaker finally assures us, choosing a word resonant with biblical promise that also describes what happens when the merest breeze lifts a feather or scrap of paper and lets it float, as we all must, on currents that carry us in ways we can neither will nor resist. The assurance is a benediction, a postscript to the Beatitudes, an assurance of the happiness that can come only from grace, and will come to all of us who are invited to cast our cares on the One who cares for us and, one day, to lay our burdens down at the feet of God, perhaps to discover that God carried the bulk of them all along.

Michael Chitwood

On Being Asked to Pray for a Van

My evangelical brethren have let me know,
via the quarterly fundraising letter,
that they can't get the gospel around
because their van has given up the ghost.
God in the machine, help them.
I lift up their carburetor and their transaxle.
Bless them with meshed gears and a greased cam shaft.
Free their lifters.
Deliver their differential
and anoint their valves and their pistons.
Unblock their engine block
and give them deep treaded tires.
Their brakes cry out to You. Hear them, O Lord.
Drive out the demons from their steering column
and come in to the transmission
that they may know the peace of passing.
Minister even unto the turn indicator.
Creator Spirit, Holy Maker of the Universe,
give them gas.

This edgy poem by Michael Chitwood, professor and editor at *Southern Cultures,* was written in 2007. It's possible to read this work as a wry comment on prayers that seem to trivialize communion with God. I've been party to occasional good-natured arguments about whether it's appropriate to pray to find a parking space or misplaced glasses. Or, worse, to get a table at a restaurant that takes no reservations. The Creator, some insist, is not likely to take an interest in self-imposed First World problems.

That point of view, which deserves recurrent consideration, might be countered by Anne Lamott's simple typology of prayer: all prayers, she suggests, are elaborations of three words: "Help, Thanks, Wow!" Prayers for help, she and others insist, may be uttered in all times and places, because we always need help, sometimes in ways we don't know enough to ask for. And we can trust the One who promised that not a sparrow would fall without the loving witness of God, who cares for all creatures and who numbered the hairs of our heads.

In this vein, I remember being touched on various occasions by a story my mother told about a surprise check that came to the mission school in South India where she and my father worked for a number of years. It covered to the penny the amount needed on that day to repair the Jeep that enabled a medical team to bring much-needed care to the villages in the area. In fact, she had several stories about "coincidences" far too precisely timed and tuned to be accidents. Later, I was similarly touched by the declaration just mentioned: the rabbi's confident assurance to the young tailor seeking a blessing for his new sewing machine: "There is a blessing for everything."

In that spirit, whatever the intentions of the poet, one may read Chitwood's prayer for a van as a model for a kind of prayer it's good to keep in our repertoire. It's a prayer to the God, as Arundhati Roy put it, "of small things." Its specificity may be taken as a measure of intimacy and trust that God is very near.

Scott Cairns's lovely poem "Draw Near" opens with a paradox that lies at the heart of faith: "For near is where you'll meet what you have wandered / far to find." Chitwood seems to suggest that "near" may be in the very guts of an exhausted van—the carburetor, the valves and pistons, the engine block. One answer to the question often asked in desperation or exasperation—"Where is God?"—is always and simply, "Here."

To specify further—here under the hood, in the machine, in the very pipes and rods human hands have made—is to reinforce the radical, even scandalous claim that God does, in fact, enter into the smallest human affairs—that divine energy whirls in every atom, and that all things lie in the Spirit's unpredictable path. I've spent many years in writing courses urging for specificity. Specificity is a measure of commitment, of attention, of the depth of knowledge one brings to the naming of objects and incidents and needs. We may, and should, pray for peace in the world in our time, but there is something more vigorous and daring about praying for peace in Aleppo or Kabul as we see on the evening news an anguished mother clutching a ragged child in the rubble. Specificity honors the ambiguities and the complexities of what is at stake. It requires of us some awareness of our own complicity in and responsibility for what we pray about.

So, to return to the broken van. The prayer responds to the invitation to ask for what we need by considering closely and thoughtfully what the need might be. The gears might need adjustment, the cam shaft grease, the tires new treads or replacements. When we pause to name our needs more carefully, we may find ourselves understanding our needs more clearly, and our role in creating them and in addressing them. Prayer is partly a practice of paying attention to what is, and partly a practice of participation. When we pray, we engage our own energies as well as inviting God's. Good prayer is rooted in good noticing. Good prayer requires its own kind of intelligent imagination.

When we bring intelligence and imagination to prayer, our relationship with God becomes richer, more interesting, and more active. Abstractions kill the spirit. Specifics demand that we enter into life and look closely at its particulars. Reformed theologians recognize that Christian faith is rooted in a "scandal of particularity," reminding us that the Incarnation itself can seem absurd to those of us whose God is too elevated for our own good. It is, of course, impossible to overestimate the magnitude and magnanimity of divine being, but it's also impossible to imagine the infinitesimal detail of the Creator's attention—to protons and electrons and sub-atomic particles, to light waves and neutrinos and nanoseconds. And, when need be, to carburetors and transaxles.

Anonymous

Truck Driver's Prayer
by a Young Ghanaian Christian

Lord,
the motor under me is running hot.
Lord,
there are twenty-eight people
and lots of luggage in the truck.
Underneath are my bad tyres.
The brakes are unreliable.
Unfortunately I have no money,
and parts are difficult to get.
Lord,
I did not overload the truck.
Lord,
'Jesus is mine'
is written on the vehicle,
for without him I would not drive
a single mile.
The people in the back are relying on me.
They trust me because they see the words:
'Jesus is mine'.
Lord,
I trust you!

First comes the straight road
with little danger,
I can keep my eyes on the women,
children and chickens in the village.
But soon the road begins to turn,
it goes up and down,
it jumps and dances,
this death-road to Kumasi.
Tractors carrying mahogany trunks drive
as if there were no right or left.
Lord,
Kumasi is the temptation
to take more people than we should.
Let's overcome it!

The road to Accra is another problem.
Truck drivers try to beat the record,
although the road is poor
and has many holes
and there are many curves
before we come to the hills.

And finally to Akwasim.
Passing large churches in every village,
I am reminded of you, and in reverence
I take off my hat.
Now downhill in second gear.

One more temptation;
the straight road to Accra.

Lord, keep my feet steady on the pedals
even on the straight road to Accra.

Lord,
I sing hallelujah
when the ride is ended
for you brought the truck and the people
in safety
through the hustle and bustle of Accra.

Lord, all is mercy,
because
'Jesus is mine'.
Hallelujah. Amen.

Now and then I assure friends who are facing a difficult encounter or an arduous trip that I will "pray them through." What I mean by that phrase is that I commit to holding them in my awareness and lifting them up in prayer during the event itself—the surgery, the performance, the difficult conversation—accompanying them as I can from a distance. When I first read this anonymous prayer-poem by a young Ghanaian Christian truck driver, tucked in among many more conventional prayers in the 1985 *Oxford Book of Prayer*, I first thought what a fine example it was of "praying through"—praying as you go, along the way, in the very course of action. It's quite a different kind of prayer from those offered in anticipation and preparation, or those offered in thanksgiving and release of results into God's hands.

Beginning with an inventory of possible and actual difficulties—a motor running hot, twenty-eight passengers and all their luggage, bad tires and unreliable brakes—the prayer reveals the driver's sense of urgency, as well as his earnestness and the intimacy of his conversation. Lest we assume that he's hoping his prayer will excuse him for negligent vehicle maintenance, he also enumerates his good-faith efforts to do what he can on limited funds. He doesn't overload the truck. He pays for what he can. But he also prays. And "Jesus is mine" is painted on his truck—a testimony, an assurance to passengers, a sign of protection, a public declaration of love.

Small refrains keep bringing the driver's darting awareness back to center. "Lord," which he repeats nine times in the course of the journey, summons attention—his, ours, and God's—back to the heart of the matter: everything depends on God. Jesus is Lord. Jesus is Love. "Jesus is mine," which he repeats three times, is an amusingly but instructively literal reminder that Jesus is the guard and guide on this journey, "for without him I would not drive / a single mile."

The driver's petitions are laced with confessions: he is tempted to take on too many passengers, to drive certain stretches too fast, to take unnecessary risks, to contend with other drivers. He knows his own weaknesses, and God knows them, too. But his confessions are imbedded in a context of loving confidence: "Jesus is mine." "Lord, / I trust you!" "All is mercy." Lifting his hat as he passes churches, he offers a prayer of continued and continuous greeting.

Indeed, this sweet, sturdy, practical prayer recalls John Calvin's much more formal one, sung still as a hymn that invites us into joyful confession and profession: "I greet thee, who my sure Redeemer art, /My only trust and Savior of my heart . . . Thou art the life by which alone we live. . . ." The driver's prayer gives us a way to imagine what it might mean that God is the life by which alone we live, our only trust, and, as Jesus promised, "with us always"—on the long stretches, past the churches and the chickens, over the potholes—a divine companion on the journey.

The metaphor of the journey is a commonplace among believers, though not, I think, a cliché. It remains apt and lively and even literal. "I'm walking down the road," one hymn reads, and others "Come travel this road," "Precious Lord, take my hand, lead me on," and "I want Jesus to walk with me." I also want Jesus to fly with me, and drive the highways where more and more hurried and harried commuters weave from one lane to another without signaling.

Wherever we are, the Psalmist assures us, God is with us—following us to "the uttermost parts of the sea" and to the depths of our own dark hearts. We can practice God's presence in cubicles and behind grocery carts and in library carrels, giving thanks as we go for small obstacles avoided, temptations overcome, potential disasters averted. Bidden or unbidden, God is present, protecting us, this lively prayer reminds us, and also, perhaps, protecting the "women, children and chickens" from us as we rattle and weave among them, praying as we go.

Known and Knowing

Psalm 139:1–12 (NRSV)

O Lord, you have searched me and known me.
2 You know when I sit down and when I rise up;
   you discern my thoughts from far away.
3 You search out my path and my lying down,
   and are acquainted with all my ways.
4 Even before a word is on my tongue,
   O Lord, you know it completely.
5 You hem me in, behind and before,
   and lay your hand upon me.
6 Such knowledge is too wonderful for me;
   it is so high that I cannot attain it.

7 Where can I go from your spirit?
   Or where can I flee from your presence?
8 If I ascend to heaven, you are there;
   if I make my bed in Sheol, you are there.
9 If I take the wings of the morning
   and settle at the farthest limits of the sea,
10 even there your hand shall lead me,
   and your right hand shall hold me fast.

11 If I say, "Surely the darkness shall cover me,
   and the light around me become night,"
12 even the darkness is not dark to you;
   the night is as bright as the day,
   for darkness is as light to you.

The Psalmist sets a gold standard for poets who pray. Though there are more and less poetic translations of the Psalms, the elegance and strength, the longing and ebullient delight survive in most of them, and have enlivened the prayers of gathered congregations for centuries. Some seem made for public prayer: "O sing to the Lord a new song!" and "Why do the nations rage?" But many speak from the depths of a single awakened heart to a God who draws near, inclines an ear, dwells in secret places, and does not forsake us. For sheer beauty, I think Psalm 139 is unsurpassed. The first twelve verses complete an arc of praise that acknowledges with sure and certain awe who God is, how intimately present and yet how far beyond the measures of the mind.

Reciting God's own attributes and acts is a curious thing to do in prayer. But as a reminder of who God is and who we are, recalling the ways that God is present to us helps us situate ourselves rightly before the One without whom there is nothing. The opening lines of the psalm let God know that I know that God knows all that is within me. "You have searched me and known me." It is a paradoxical truth, both unsettling and reassuring. It dissolves any illusion I may harbor that I can keep my darkest secrets hidden or maintain my social respectability before God. Naked came I, and naked I stand before the Holy One.

There's something touching in the attentiveness of a God who pays attention to when I sit down and when I rise up, and in the patience of a God who seeks me out and waits through the night, and who listens for words, knowing full well what I am likely to say. This God "hems me in"—hovering, touching, impinging, minding my business, supporting me even when I'm not aware I need it. The multiplication of active verbs in this canticle of amazement prevents us from flattening God into an idol or image or icon. We are not the actors or viewers, but the acted upon. The Psalmist worships not from an aesthetic distance, but from within the very heart of an embrace. Reciting the psalm, we become aware that we, too, are held and witnessed and accompanied and loved.

In verse 7 the tone becomes slightly darker: "Where can I go from your spirit? Or where can I flee from your presence?" The words are not comforting: the speaker imagines being pursued, found out, sought out, met and surprised and sometimes ambushed on his escape route. I find it hard to read these verses without remembering Francis Thompson's strange, haunting, audacious poem, "The Hound of Heaven," where God is likened to a hound seeking out the fugitive soul with dogged, unflagging persistence, trained to his purpose of pursuit and not to be swayed from it. It starts this way:

> I fled Him, down the nights and down the days;
> I fled Him, down the arches of the years;
> I fled Him, down the labyrinthine ways
>   Of my own mind; and in the mist of tears
> I hid from Him, and under running laughter.

The image of being pursued in this way isn't entirely reassuring, even if it is by One who is finally identified as a "tremendous Lover." Thompson knows, and the Psalmist knows, that the love of God is as fierce as it is tender.

My favorite lines of the psalm, and the ones that seem to me most mysterious and poetic, are these:

> If I take the wings of the morning
> and settle at the farthest limits of the sea,
> even there your hand shall lead me,
> and your right hand shall hold me fast.

Even in our most desperate attempts at escape, we are led and held by the very One we seek to evade. The King James Version gives us the phrase "the uttermost parts of the sea." When I learned that passage as a child, that place seemed far more remote and strange than "the farthest limits." And "the wings of the morning" hardly bears comment, so sufficient is its mysterious beauty, except that it evokes the flight of a seabird soaring at dawn.

Remember, the Psalmist tells us, with an immediacy that dissolves the millennia between us, the unimaginable immanence of God. Remember how present God's help is in time of trouble. Remember that you are held and guided, even as you wander and sink and flail. Remember that you cannot hide, that you will not be abandoned, and that, though it is "a fearful thing to fall into the hands of the living God," only there can you "lie down in peace and sleep" in the presence of the One who, alone, makes us dwell in safety.

Praying with Poems,
Praying through Poems:
An Afterword

Poetry, as we see, can open pathways into prayer. Sometimes we will find in a poem the prayer we need for the moment, and that poem can simply be received and recited gratefully, traveling from the poet's heart to ours to God's. Sometimes the words or phrases we encounter in a poem trigger associations that open new avenues of reflection or awareness: we wouldn't have thought to put it just that way. We may also find in poems echoes or amplifications or correctives or provocations to look further, to ask new questions, to stay through the dry times, to enter our places of darkness unafraid.

In the following few pages I offer a number of practices for integrating poetry and prayer, allowing poets to become our "prayer partners" in a sense. It is my hope that both the poems in this book, which are either written as prayers or written explicitly about prayer, and whatever other poems you discover and are drawn to can become occasions of grace.

If, as I believe, words have a sacramental dimension in their actual capacity to heal, forgive, open the heart, and bring about change, we need to cultivate reading practices—attentive, mindful, intentional, informed—that allow us to receive the gifts they offer. As you encounter poems, perhaps beginning with those gathered here, try any of the following exercises and see what doors they open.

May your reading hours be blessed, and may all you come to know by heart bring you nearer to the heart of God.

Collect a few favorite words, phrases, lines, or images from a poem. Pause over what you've noticed and consider what drew you there. Allow one of those to become an anchoring word or phrase in a few minutes of centering prayer. Or write a prayer that emerges from and incorporates those words.

Find the places where you find yourself saying "Yes!" Consider what it is you're affirming, assenting, or consenting to—how the poem opens a way to a deeper awareness of what you may need to pause over, recognize, and consent to.

Choose one image from a poem written before the twentieth century that seems strange or surprising to you. Do you find yourself welcoming or resisting it? What other images does it generate? Use it as the central image for a poem of your own. Notice where the image takes you, what it opens up that may have been closed.

Reflect on how a poem from an earlier century connects you to the long lineage of believers. Receive it as one message from the great communion of saints.

In a time of sorrow, read a poem or a psalm about sorrow and write a list of verbs or verb phrases entitled "What sorrow does." As the list grows, see which of those verbs deepens your awareness of the dimensions of grief or loss or mourning. As the list develops, you might turn it into a litany, laying each experience of sorrow before God for healing.

Choose a line from a poem or a psalm as an epigraph for a poem or written prayer of your own.

Carry a single poem with you for a week, taking it out to look at when, for instance, you're standing in line or waiting for the gas tank to fill, or at times when you might be inclined to pull out your phone or riffle through magazines in the check-out line. At the end of the week, see how much of it you know by heart. See what little shoots of feeling and growth it's produced—how, for instance, it's fostered gratitude or awareness of God's presence or hope.

Learn by heart a prayer from a previous century, paying attention to how antique words open unfamiliar pathways of reflection or reframe a particular faith experience.

Write a short poem about your own interior space, considering "where" you go when you meditate or pray in architectural, geographical, or geological terms.

Choose a poem for your own funeral and write a short explanation of your choice to those who may have to organize it. Emphasize words or phrases in the poem that you hope to leave as part of your legacy of faith.

Compose another verse to a favorite hymn.

Write three haiku without moving from where you are, taking in something about this moment, this visual field, these sounds, this place, letting this be an experiment in being fully present.

Consider how a particular poem brings you into the present—how you breathe with it, how it invites your attention, how it quiets or restores you to yourself. Write a few lines in answer to the call of this moment, the feeling of this moment, the choices offered in this moment.

Pray in dialogue with a poem, in "call and response" fashion, pausing after each line or two to speak or write a prayer that the poem evokes or allows.

Works Cited

Alarcón, Francisco X. "L.A. Prayer." In *From the Other Side of Night / Del otro lado de la noche: New and Selected Poems.* Tucson: University of Arizona Press, 2002.

Anonymous. "Truck Driver's Prayer (by a young Ghanaian Christian)." In *The Oxford Book of Prayer*, ed. George Appleton, pp. 127-29. Oxford: Oxford University Press, 1985.

Berry, Wendell. "Prayer after Eating." In *New Collected Poems*, p. 169. Berkeley: Counterpoint Press, 2013.

Bingen, Hildegard von. "I am the one whose praise echoes on high." In *Meditations with Hildegard of Bingen*, ed. Gabriele Uhlein, p. 31. Rochester, VT: Bear & Company, 1983.

Cairns, Scott. "Possible Answers to Prayer." In *Compass of Affection: Poems, New and Selected*, p. 91. Brewster, MA: Paraclete Press, 2006.

Chitwood, Michael. "On Being Asked to Pray for a Van." In *Spill*. North Adams, MA: Tupelo Press, 2007.

Clifton, Lucille. "spring song." In *The Collected Poems of Lucille Clifton*. Rochester, NY: BOA Editions, 1987.

Donne, John. "Holy Sonnet XIV." In *John Donne: The Complete English Poems*. London: Penguin Books, 1971.

Eliot, T. S. "The Dry Salvages." In *Four Quartets*. Boston, MA: Mariner Books, Houghton Mifflin Harcourt, 1968.

Frost, Robert. "A Prayer in Spring." In *The Poetry of Robert Frost: The Collected Poems, Complete and Unabridged*. New York: Henry Holt & Co., 1979.

Harjo, Joy. "Eagle Poem." In *In Mad Love and War*. Middletown, CT: Wesleyan University Press, 1990.

Herbert, George. "The Call." In *George Herbert: The Complete English Poems*. London: Penguin Books, 1991.

Hopkins, Gerard Manley. "Thou Art Indeed Just, Lord." In *Gerard Manley Hopkins: Poems and Prose*. London: Penguin Books, 1953.

Kamienska, Anna. "Those Who Carry." In *Astonishments: Selected Poems of Anna Kamienska*, ed. and trans. Grażyna Drabik and David Curzon. Brewster, MA: Paraclete Press, 2007.

Kinnell, Galway. "Prayer." In *The Past*. Boston, MA: Mariner Books, Houghton Mifflin Harcourt, 1985.

Levertov, Denise. "The Avowal." In *The Stream and the Sapphire*. Cambridge, MA: New Directions, 1997.

Merton, Thomas. "The Candlemas Procession." In *The Collected Poems of Thomas Merton*. Cambridge, MA: New Directions, 1977.

Oliver, Mary. "Praying" In *Thirst*. Boston: Beacon Press, 2006.

SAID. "Psalm." In *99 Psalms*, trans. Mark Burrows. Brewster, MA: Paraclete Press, 2013.

Smith, Walter Chalmers. "Immortal, Invisible, God Only Wise." In *The Presbyterian Hymnal*. Louisville: Westminster John Knox Press, 1990.

Sorescu, Marin. "Prayer." In *My Hands Behind My Back*, trans. Gabriela Dragnea, Stuart Friebert, and Adriana Varga. Oberlin, OH: Oberlin College Press, 1991.

Wilbur, Richard. "The Eye." In *Richard Wilbur: Collected Poems, 1943-2004*. Boston, MA: Mariner Books, Houghton Mifflin Harcourt, 2006.

List of Permissions

Francisco X. Alarcón, "L.A. Prayer." From *From the Other Side of Night / Del otro lado de la noche* by Francisco X. Alarcón. Copyright © 2002 Francisco X. Alarcón. Reprinted by permission of the University of Arizona Press.

Wendell Berry, "Prayer after Eating." From *The Selected Poems of Wendell Berry.* Copyright © 1998 by Wendell Berry. Reprinted by permission of Counterpoint Press.

Scott Cairns, "Possible Answers to Prayer." From *Compass of Affection: Poems New and Selected* by Scott Cairns. Copyright © 2006 by Scott Cairns. Used by permission of Paraclete Press: www.paracletepress.com.

Michael Chitwood, "On Being Asked to Pray for a Van." From *Spill*, published by Tupelo Press. Copyright © 2007 by Michael Chitwood. Used with permission.

Richard Wilbur, excerpt from "The Eye." From *The Mind-Reader* by Richard Wilbur. Copyright © 1972 by Richard Wilbur. Reprinted by permission of Houghton Mifflin Harcourt Publishing Company. All rights reserved.